Moreton Frewen

The Economic Crisis

Moreton Frewen

The Economic Crisis

ISBN/EAN: 9783337378196

Printed in Europe, USA, Canada, Australia, Japan

Cover: Foto ©Suzi / pixelio.de

More available books at **www.hansebooks.com**

BY
MORETON FREWEN,
B.A. TRINITY COLLEGE, CAMB.

LONDON:
KEGAN PAUL, TRENCH AND CO.
1, PATERNOSTER SQUARE.
1888.

DEDICATED

TO

THE AUTHOR OF

"𝔗𝔥𝔢 𝔖𝔦𝔩𝔳𝔢𝔯 𝔓𝔬𝔲𝔫𝔡."

PREFACE.

WHILE in India last winter I wrote for the *Pioneer* a series of articles on the Economic Crisis. It has been suggested to me to republish these in book form, and this I have now ventured to do, because, however incomplete as a statement of the present currency conditions, I hope that at least it may possess some value as coming within the comprehension of the average reader.

The first ten chapters are republished from the *Pioneer* with but few alterations; the concluding chapter on "The Socialism of Tomorrow" has not been published elsewhere. It is intended as a timely protest against the dogmas of the individualist school of writers, and to show that there is an alternative neither unscientific nor necessarily uneconomical, if the excesses of that gigantic "sweating system," induced by unrestricted competition, and now so universally obtaining, are found to admit of no remedy short of State intervention.

CONTENTS.

CHAPTER I.

DEPRESSION OF PRICES BY LEGISLATION.

Universal prosperity resulting from Californian and Australian Gold supplies—Mr. Disraeli on the effects of recent monetary legislation—Mr. Goschen in agreement as to cause of depression—The Money Famine—The "Quantity" Theory—Hume—J. S. Mill—Rapid growth of political intelligence in the United States and the victory of the "Silver men"—Increasing tyranny of the Money Power in Europe—Simultaneous legislation in 1883 to demonetize Silver—As showing effect of similar legislation on prices—Analogy of change of values of beef and mutton—The enrichment of the few by the impoverishment of the many ... ... p. 1

CHAPTER II.

THE BLAND BILL.

Widespread educational results following from agitation over Bland Act—Interest of Europe in the continuance of this Act—Mr. Evarts at Paris Conference—Mr. Goschen at Manchester in 1885—The real Silver Crisis was in 1884—Triumph of Anti-Contraction Party in the United States—Surreptitious demonetization of silver at Washington in 1873—Why it escaped notice—Exactly similar reasons permitted Lord Liverpool's legislation in 1816—Resumption of specie payments in England—Mr. Western and Mr. Attwood in 1822 on the cause of the sufferings of the agricultural interest—Warning to Congress to resume specie payments on basis

x   CONTENTS.

not of one, but of both metals—Bland Act vetoed by President Hayes—But repassed by a two-thirds majority in Congress—Entire collapse of "law of Gresham" as understood by the Wall Street economists—Extraordinary sustained attack in English press upon the *bona fides* of Congressional majority—Bland Bill merely an effective makeshift, awaiting finality ... ... p. 10

CHAPTER III.

PRICES.

Short history of prices—Historical interdependence of volume of money and prices—Steady *rise* of all prices for a thousand years, *pari passu*, with mechanical improvements—Alison on Californian discoveries—His bright expectations not verified, consequence of anti-Silver legislation—Disinberison of Silver—Prices and the currency before and after discovery of America—Potosi—Jacob's history of precious metals—His recognition of currency conditions which theoretically should have depressed prices—But the discovery left to Newmarch and Jevons that this fall of prices had actually taken place—"Over-production" theory—Years between 1830 and 1850 were years of maximum "cheapness," of maximum distress also—Mr. Disraeli on the situation in 1832—Opportune gold discoveries in California in 1845—The "Golden Age"—Index numbers, Soetbeer—Jevons—*Economist*—England's stock of legal tender money in 1878, 1884, 1888—Lord Iddesleigh's Royal Commission—M. Sauerbeck's index numbers—Are we returning to the prices of the 15th century? ... ... p. 24

CHAPTER IV.

FALL OF PRICES.

Fall of prices according to Messrs. Fowler, Mulhall and Wells—Their theory enormously emphasizes the importance of guarding against a currency contraction—Otherwise entirely irrelevant—Mistakes of Mr. Wells—Mr. Mulhall on ratio of metallic money to business done—Increase of banking system may even require increase of metallic money—

Mr. Wells on gold deficiency—Importance of statistical accuracy—Mr. Wells' misconstruction of statements of MM. Cernuschi and Sauerbeck—Lower freight charges may either be the cause or the effect of lower prices—Jevons on the depreciation of Gold—Probable direction of future legislation ... ... p. 37

CHAPTER V.

MR. DAVID A. WELLS ON "BIMETALLISM."

Bimetallism omitted from his inquiry—Chevalier's testimony that the automatic action of French bimetallism was the parachute which broke the fall of Gold, and thus prevented in gold countries a catastrophic rise of all prices—Mr. Wells on the automatic action—Admits however the recent steadiness of Silver as a measure of prices—Therefore Gold has appreciated, not Silver depreciated—Fall of price of Silver must induce fall of wheat prices—The Hindoo riot and the interests of the English and American farmer—"Perversity" of rupee—Conclusion derived from Mr. Wells' mistakes—Science of statistics inductive—But economic science why analytical and deductive—Mental method of statisticians probably defective—Importance of statistical accuracy ... ... p. 56

CHAPTER VI.

NATIONAL DEBTS AND THE GROWTH OF SOCIALISM.

What is National Debt—National debts actually though not nominally increase their burden with every fall of prices—Amount of our National Debt measured in wheat at the time the debt was being contracted—National Debt of the United States—Its rapid *dollar* reduction—But its persistent increase in terms of commodities—Argument of the bondholder refuted—Premium on his patriotism measured by the premium on Gold—That almost the entire amount of taxation is deducted from that share of production which is paid to Labour—Lord Derby on the coming Repudiation—The argument that being a creditor Nation, England profits by appreciation of Gold—Turkey's reply to this—

Violation of contract involved in the National Debt—Non-responsibility to the State, of mere owners of gold as compared with owners of other forms of fixed capital—The Appreciation of Gold and the Egyptian finances—British treatment of a similar disease in Ireland and Egypt—Prospective emergence of Socialism, on a scientific basis p. 70

CHAPTER VII.

THE TWO GROUPS OF "BIMETALLISTS."

Misapplication of the term "Bimetallist"—Reformers favour Unity of Standard, but monometallists favour two distinct Standards within one Empire, one in England, the other in India—Inconvenience of the two standard system increases as the distance increases—Profits of Trade depend on such subjective causes as a speech from Mr. Goschen—Buying "forward exchange" a costly form of Insurance against risk—Alleged differences of opinion amongst bimetallists accounted for—Two distinct standpoints—Those who merely assert Mills' quantity theory, and those who attach the greater importance to the dislocation of the par of exchange—A "Gold question" and a "Silver question"—Issue of pound notes, inoperative *qua* prices, mischievous in this, that they would displace and drive out Gold—Cernuschi's attitude ... ... p. 81

CHAPTER VIII.

THE FIXED RATIO—IS IT PRACTICABLE?

Origin of word "pecunia" (pecus) the legal tender of Cattle—Why impossible that State could establish ratio between value of sheep and cattle—Cost of production decides such values—But not so the precious metals—Cost of production of Gold or Silver greater than value when produced—How this can be—Gambling propensity inherent in human nature—Leadville—Comstock Mine—Within what limits therefore is it in the power of the State to fix ratio—Suggested between one to seven, and one to thirty—Wolowski on importance of Money—But what should ratio be? ... p. 90

CHAPTER IX.

THE FIXED RATIO—ITS PROPORTION.

Sudden considerable disturbance of ratio, twice only in six hundred years—To be referred each time to monetary legislation at (1) Venice about 1290, (2) in Berlin in 1873—Alterations in comparative supplies of precious metals, *inter se*, have never considerably affected ratio—How to restore ratio without injustice—M. Cernuschi—Silver legal tender in terms of Gold—Clearly thereafter Silver could never fall—Reason why it would immediately rise—Automatic action of bimetallism—Neither metal can fall if given prerogative of legal tender—Therefore *inter se* neither metal can rise—Finality of 1 to $15\frac{1}{2}$ established by legislation now hundreds of years old—The "Warner compromise"—Endorsed by Earl Grey ... ... p. 99

CHAPTER X.

INDIA AND THE SILVER QUESTION.

The stimulus afforded by a falling exchange to exports of wheat and yarns from India—The position of the Bombay Cotton Industry—Mr. J. G. Scott on the conditions of cotton manufacture in Bombay—Stimulus, however, merely affects export Trade of India, which is only five per cent. total commerce of India—Increased taxation and uncertainties in all trades—*Quarterly Review* on the production of wheat—Mr. Edward Atkinson—Brisk railway construction by immense expenditure locally, has served to raise local prices in the wheat growing States of America, and thus to protect them from agricultural collapse—By diminishing wheat cultivation, production of meat has been stimulated in the United States, consequently increased competition and fall of prices in Ireland 108

CHAPTER XI.

INDIA AND THE SILVER QUESTION (*continued*).

Prodigies of modern production—Consequence of (1) improved modern machinery, (2) cheap loanable capital—Cheap capital enables modern manufacturer to operate profitably with very low margin of profits—Present difficulty of exchange is checking flow of capital from England to India, and thus makes borrowing rates in India artificially high—Consequences of the Economic Crisis in England and India summed up ... ... p. 119

CHAPTER XII.'

DEPRECIATED CURRENCIES AND THEIR EFFECT ON PRICES.

The Russian currency—Mr. Harris on imported wheat—Argument of Mr. Harris considered—Remedy for increasing premium on Gold, to restore Silver everywhere to legal tender—Interest of Germany in Russian finances—Depreciating currencies, however stimulating to export trades, destructive of domestic trade and of foreign credit—Argentine finances—Rapidity of variations in gold agio—Profitable exchange operations in consequence of these variations ... ... p. 125

CHAPTER XIII.

THE SOCIALISM OF TO-MORROW.

Socialism and the future of legislation—Socialism not necessarily unscientific—Extension of Franchise has deprived middle classes of paramount influence—Working classes have little to fear from experimental legislation—A form of Socialism which is not anti-social—Not re-distribution but a more equitable distribution in future—Success of the State Post Office—The State an efficient "middle man"—Production the domain of the individual, distribution the domain of the State—The State not in sympathy with "the masses." Why?—The State ownership of railways—An incident of a recent "rate war" in the United States—Cost of purchase practically a "conversion" scheme—Elimination of brokers and other commission agents—Moment for such changes opportune in United States—Utilize surplus revenue—Industrial aspects—Social and moral aspects—The tyranny of "Rings" of middle men—Only remediable if railways in the hands of the State—State purchase of Banks—Bagehot's inquiries as to profit of banking—Present profits of London Joint Stock Banks would rapidly redeem our National Debt—Banking even now subject to frequent State interference—Injustice of Peel's Act of 1844—Lord George Bentinck on Peel's Act—Land Socialism uneconomical until a better distribution of products is secured—State regulation of hours of labour—Free Trade was a remedy devised in the interests of the middle classes—Which classes should most fairly be called on to emigrate, middle men or working men? —Limitation of State functions. Where?—Limited Liability principle failure, except in cases where State could operate more profitably still—Bagehot on the Joint Stock principle —Bismarck and Industrial Insurance Offices—Profits of Insurance Companies—The Credit of the State is so much better than that of the individual that the entire revenue might be derived from the State Credit—Political aspects of State Socialism—Example of France—Our present experience of State control—The Professors and *laissez faire*— Value of legislative decentralization, but of industrial centralization—Value of a distinct political issue—The demands from below inevitable ... ... p. 131

APPENDIX.

THE ECONOMIC DISTURBANCES SINCE 1873 ... p. 165

(Reprinted from the *New York Commercial Chronicle*.)

THE ECONOMIC CRISIS.

I.

THE DEPRESSION OF PRICES BY LEGISLATION.

MORE than eight years ago a writer in the *Edinburgh Review* closed a very elaborate statement of the social and industrial effects of the great gold discoveries in California and Australia, with these words: "The world has come to the close of a very memorable epoch: the present generation has seen come and go the most remarkable outburst of material prosperity which has ever visited the nations of mankind. The epoch has been short-lived as a northern summer, and the world has fallen into winter again; but a large portion of the fruits of the golden summer enduringly remain a rich heritage for subsequent generations."

At the time those lines were written the connection between the prevalent high range of prices and gold "cheap," because abundant, was little considered, except by a few professors of the "dismal science;" the collapse of all prices which has since taken place, and which has produced not only in Ireland but in America and on the European continent, such an extraordinary social upheaval, could not at that time have been foreseen by the writer, nor had the question of the legal tender position of silver and the agitation over the Bland Bill become, as to-day, the chief political issue in the great Republic of the Western Hemisphere. Almost alone among our public men Mr. Disraeli appears to have foreseen the troubles which were to follow from the effect of recent monetary legislation on prices. Speaking at Glasgow in November 1873, just after the change of her standard by Germany, to which I shall refer later, Mr. Disraeli said:—

"I attribute the monetary disturbance which has occurred, and is now to a certain extent acting very injuriously upon trade, I attribute it to the great changes which the Governments of Europe are making in reference to their standard of value. Our gold standard is not the cause of our commercial prosperity, but the consequence of that prosperity. It is quite evident that we must prepare ourselves for great convulsions in the money market, not occasioned by speculation or any of the old causes which have been alleged, but by a new cause with which we are not sufficiently acquainted."

Six years later, in March 1879, when the monetary morbus had become evident, Mr. Disraeli, then Lord Beaconsfield, said:—

"All this time the produce of the gold mines of Australia and California has been regularly diminishing, and the consequence is that, while these great alterations on the continent in favour of a gold currency have been made, notwithstanding that increase of population which alone requires a considerable increase of currency to carry on its transactions, the amount of the currency itself is yearly diminishing, until a state of affairs has been brought about by gold production exactly the reverse of that which it produced at first. Gold is every day appreciating in value, and as it appreciates the lower become prices. It is not impossible that, as affairs develop, the country may require that some formal investigation should be made of the causes which are affecting the value of the precious metals—and the effect which the change in the value of the precious metals has upon the industries of the country, and upon the continual fall of prices."

Lord Beaconfield's view thus expressed, that prices were falling not because of any general over-production of commodities, but because of a rapid local diminution of the supply of that precious metal which measures values, was accepted at once by Mr. Goschen, one of the ablest financiers of the age. The production of gold from the mines was known to be diminishing; its yearly consumption in the arts and manufactures had increased, till it was now nearly seventy per cent. of the entire annual yield, and coming on the top of these causes of appreciation, two great nations, Germany and the United States, had discarded, the one her silver money, the other paper money, and had come to market to buy gold instead. Their purchases of gold have been on such a vast scale, that to-day these two nations are retaining more than a quarter of all the gold currency of the world. To use M. de Laveleye's words, gold like water being now spread over a larger area has lowered its level at its original basin. If concurrently with an immense new demand for bread, the wheat harvest of the world was for several years a failure, surely bread would be very dear, and in the same way an increased demand for gold, side by side with supplies rapidly diminishing, has brought about a gold famine which shows itself more and more every day in a constant shrinkage of prices. More cotton or wheat, more labour or land, must be given for gold because gold is scarce. The statesmen having satisfied themselves that such was the origin of the growing financial disorder, we were induced to turn to our school-books to find that Cairnes, Newmarch, Jevons and a score of others writers were in complete agreement. Hume more than a century since wrote: "Suppose four-fifths of all the money in Britain to be annihilated in one night. Must not the price of all labour and commodities sink in proportion?" More emphatic still is John Stuart Mill's statement of the "quantity theory." "That an increase of the quantity of money," wrote Mill, "raises prices, and a diminution lowers them, is the most elementary proposition in the theory of currency, and without it we should have no key to any of the others." But where eight years since a few students and professors understood the significance of the "Silver question," to-day the subject is attracting the intelligent interest of ten thousand business men. In the United States, where, under the tutelage of manhood suffrage, a very advanced condition of political enlightenment has been arrived at, the so-called "Silver men," the opponents of a contracted currency, have simply swept the field from Maine to California, from Puget Sound to the Gulf of Mexico. It is now recognized in America that the money power may become a most dangerous tyranny, and that in Europe it is this power, wielded to-day by half a dozen financial houses, which controls to an ever-increasing extent the legislatures of Europe, which directs the movements of armies, and was even beginning to make its influence felt in the lobbies of the Capitol at Washington. Gold was appreciating from natural causes, from a falling-off in the output of the mines; as the sovereign became more valuable, those who either owned, or had loaned sovereigns, were becoming richer, while the debtor classes of the communities were suffering. The man who had borrowed a sovereign when it represented only a week's work, was to return it when it required the labour of ten days to procure it. But as if the natural causes for the appreciation of gold were not sufficient, class legislation of a most complex and insidious kind was now to be secured in order to bring about a further fall of prices, and a further impoverishment of the industrious; if silver could be deprived of its legal tender position as a money metal, then the work previously done by silver would have to be done by gold, all property measured by the gold standard would be shorn of half of its value, and bankers and bondholders would see their fortunes double in a day. The agitation for the repeal of the Bland Bill in 1883 and 1884 was intended to supplement the monetary legislation at Berlin in 1873; Germany was formerly, as India is to-day, on a silver basis, but legislation had been procured so that Germany had sold her silver *en masse*, and bought gold with it. This artificial demand for gold was every day driving gold to a famine price, while forcing down the price of all other commodities. If only it were possible to arrange similar legislation in the United States, so that fifty millions sterling more of legal tender silver could be pitched upon the world's silver market and sold for gold, then, while the price of the rupee might fall towards sixpence, the value of every sovereign to buy land, labour or any commodity would be doubled; those debtor classes of the community who owed fixed amounts of gold would be insolvent, their creditors the "Gold Bugs," according to the current phraseology in America, would become the universal owners! Is it any wonder that a nation which had shed blood like water to emancipate black men was found to recoil from legislation which aimed at the enslavement of nine-tenths of the white community for the benefit of the other tenth.

The currency problem is supposed even by many intelligent men to be so dismal and inscrutable, that even the doctors disagree over fixed ratios and other subtleties. As regards the main issue, however, the question of two legal tenders or one—the question of money cheap or money dear—the question whether the burden of all debt, national or private, is to be aggravated by anti-silver legislation—this question is, in its broader aspects, clear to the most ordinary intelligence. Silver and gold have been produced for a thousand years for purpose of legal tender money; cattle and sheep have been produced for food. If we substitute the meats for the metals, the analogy holds good; legislation is demanded which will prohibit the consumption of mutton, because, then, as mutton becomes worthless, beef will rise to a famine price, and the cattle owners will become suddenly wealthy at the expense, not merely of the owners of sheep, but of the general community. To carry the analogy further: this job was to be contrived at a time when cattle were unusually scarce and sheep more than usually numerous. Such a process—the enrichment of the few by the impoverishment of the many—had been successfully inaugurated by the monetary legislation of Germany in 1873; a new and unexpected demand for gold had been created by law; prices were falling because the value of gold was rising; gold owners and mortgagees were in clover; it was only now necessary to achieve similar legislation at Washington, and such a collapse of prices would be brought about that the bondholder, the banker, the mortgagee, would be in complete possession of the redistributed assets of the entire communities! And this fresh raid on silver in the United States only failed to achieve a similar success and a similar result, because no sufficient allowance had been made both for the general intelligence of the American community, and for its prompt recognition of the sinister nature of the proposals. The bird itself was wary and the net was set in full view.

II.

THE BLAND BILL.

WITHOUT some consideration of this Act of 1878, which takes its name from Mr. Richard Bland, a member of Congress from the State of Missouri, it would be hardly possible to make clear from what an acute monetary crisis the world has escaped, and from what dangers the business community have been saved, if indeed there is safety to-day.

And, too, from the political passions roused by this Bill, one invaluable result has followed, a result which neither its sponsors nor its opponents contemplated. Not in the United States merely, but eastward beyond the Atlantic, and westward across the Pacific, entire communities have been educated by the struggle at Washington to the recognition, that currency laws are not of local but of international importance; that prices universally can be made the mere football of the Legislatures, rising as the volume of legal tender is expanded by legislation, falling as it is contracted; and that on account of this interdependence of prices all the world over, great nations, England, France, India, have an interest not less, but I think on the contrary much greater, in the continuance, or the repeal, of the Bland Act, than have the Americans themselves. At the close of the last International Monetary Conference in Paris in 1881, when all the other Great Powers represented there were in favour of concerted action to make silver legal tender money, while England alone held aloof, Senator William Evarts, of the United States Commission, said to the representatives of Great Britain: "Very well, gentlemen, you will soon learn that *this is not Uncle Sam's funeral*," and in 1885 Mr. Goschen, when addressing the Manchester Chamber of Commerce, frankly admitted that any statement as to the future prospects of the Lancashire cotton industry was mere guess work, until the then active agitation for the repeal of the Bland Bill was in one way or the other decided. It was a great black cloud this, in the West, a cloud with a silver lining. If it broke, the exchange value of the rupee would fall to a shilling, while half Lancashire was unemployed, and trade between the East and the West paralyzed, pending a slow—an infinitely slow—process by which prices might re-adjust themselves to the altered state of the exchanges. I think, therefore, that history will later take the view that the crisis of the "Battle of the Standards" must not be referred back to Lord Liverpool's Act, which in 1816 first degraded silver from its legal tender prerogative, not even to the action of Germany in 1873, when, the pockets of that nation being stuffed with the French war indemnity, paid in gold, she sought to strike down that silver standard which had helped to carry her to Paris. These were not the real crises, though they directly led up to it. And similarly the efforts of Wolowski, Cernuschi, of Arendt and Haupt, and of Laveleye, to awaken public opinion on the Continent, of Seyd and Grenfell, of Samuel Smith and Gibbs, to whom chiefly it is owing that the present silver party in England has been collected —these were not the efforts which principally availed to prevent a monetary collapse. The real fight has been fought at Washington; I believe it has been won, and to my mind there is nothing so encouraging, pointing as it does the direction of universal progress, when other nations also shall have been educated by the possession of the franchise, as the way in which the mass of the American electorate has pronounced itself upon this subject,—a subject at once the most complex and the most momentous of existing political issues. The battle has been the battle of long hours of labour, at low wages, *versus* short hours, at full wages; the battle of a faulty distribution of wealth, mere gold collected in a few hands, against a wider and a more equitable distribution —a battle where the forces of avarice allied with ignorance had decided to increase the burden of all national debt and fixed debt, by securing a huge "unearned increment" in the purchase power of gold. Such was the nature of the conflict won by the Congress of 1884 against the united front of the banking houses of New England, against the active partisan opposition of the officials in the Government department, against nearly the entire Press of the Eastern States, and against the dictum of the President-Elect; and it was not only won but won handsomely. The silver men controlling the Central States of the Union, the West and the "Solid South" were found to constitute a full two-thirds of the Lower House, and a large majority of the Senate.

A few words now as to the Bland Act itself. In 1873, the United States currency being still dominated by the immense paper issues—"greenbacks"—the relict of the late war, gold and silver had left the country, or at least, were never seen. Germany the previous year had struck down silver, and the same thing was now to be effected in the United States. The manner in which this demonetization was brought about is very curious reading. Congress had agreed to a mere abstract proposal that, for the sake of public convenience, the various Mint laws should be codified. The silver dollar had, up to that time, been always and everywhere legal tender, and was expressed as such in all the old Mint statutes. Was it by accident or design that the new Code *omitted all mention of the silver dollar* as one of the coins which the Secretary of the Treasury might allow to be coined? The old laws, thus mutilated in codifying, were passed heedlessly through Congress, and it was not till President Grant's signature had been given that the nation awoke to the fact that the "dollar of the fathers" had, all unknown to it, been legislated out of existence. Whether the important omission was fraudulent or was really accidental, will no doubt be made clear at some later day. Senator Beck of Kentucky has declared repeatedly that Grant detected the fraud when too late, and admitted that he had been tricked into giving his signature.

It is extremely important to bear in mind that Lord Liverpool and the English Parliament in 1816 were in a position precisely similar to that occupied by President Grant and Congress in 1873. Each nation had at the time suspended specie payments, and under these circumstances the "outlawry of silver" by legislation failed to attract the attention of the constituencies, because it involved no present and visible change. The legislation was *prospective* only; in both cases it merely said: "When the time does come that we resume specie payments, then we will employ gold, and gold alone, as legal tender money." England heedlessly permitted Parliament to do this deed in 1816, ignorant of the consequences to follow later, just as the United States permitted Congress to demonetize silver in 1873. In England *the resumption of specie payments on a gold basis* had been the signal for an immense fall of prices and for universal sufferings. Mr. Western said in a debate in the House of Commons in July, 1822, that as a consequence of resuming specie payments "two-thirds of the cultivators of the soil have, in the course of a few years, and in a time of profound peace, been rendered insolvent. The turn of the landlords will soon come; they must also be involved in the ruin of their tenantry." In the course of the same debate Mr. Attwood said:—"Either all the productions of all industry have suddenly increased, which it is impossible to believe; or, otherwise, from whatever cause, a reduction in the amount of the money generally in circulation has taken place." England endured the sufferings, consequent on Lord Liverpool's blunder, and struggled on until, in the very nick of time, the great gold discoveries brought relief. The new gold has now been absorbed; has gone to other lands; has disappeared from England's currency, and from this cause she has again, since 1880, commenced to struggle and to suffer.

But not so the United States. That country had for a warning the example of our distress in the years between 1820 and 1850, and the nation was immediately awakened to the dangers which threatened it. The bondholders and other goldowners meant that specie payments should be resumed through the intermediary of *gold alone*, and keeping this in view the full significance of the Act of 1873 was at once apparent. Legislation had been smuggled through Congress; but what Congress had done, that Congress could reverse. The nation was anxious to resume specie payments, but on the basis of two legal tenders, not one. The producers of the community were not prepared to permit the price of all produce to collapse, and the burden of every fixed debt to be doubled in order that a handful of "Gold Bugs" should build their palaces on Fifth Avenue. Silver had been demonetized by stealth. The "dollar of the fathers" had been removed from its niche. It should at once be brought back again.

Mr. Bland himself at that time was, and to-day is, an advocate of unlimited free coinage of silver; that silver should in the United States be placed on precisely the same footing as gold; but such a measure, then as now, was regarded by many of the silver party as too heroic. Mr. Bland's Bill was accordingly modified by the amendment of Mr. Allison, and the "Allison-Bland Bill," as the measure was formerly called, passed both Chambers. The Act declared the standard dollar of $412\frac{1}{2}$ grains to be again legal tender, and, although unlimited coinage was not permitted, the Act provided that the Treasury should buy silver bullion for coinage to the amount of not less than two million and not more than four million dollars per month. The Bill passed, but was at once vetoed by President Hayes. According to the Constitution of the United States, the veto of the President is absolute, unless confronted by a two-thirds majority of both Houses: the Bland Bill thereupon went back to Congress, and having secured the requisite two-thirds majority became the law of the land over the veto of the President. And what has been the result?

The wiseacres of the Wall Street Banks; the leader-writers for financial papers; the City editors of leading journals, assured the American legislators, in the first place, that they were fools, that it was time for them to be taught that there was a "law of Gresham" as inevitable as the law of gravitation, which decreed that legal tender coins composed of cheaper bullion would drive out legal tender coins composed of that bullion, which at the Mint rating was the more valuable. The coinage of the Bland dollars was at the ratio of 1 of gold to 16 of silver, whereas the market price of the metals was then as 1 to 18. Silver, therefore, would surely drive out gold, and the issue of these "dishonest dollars," these "bogus dollars," these "pot-lid dollars," was to be the signal for the collapse of the growing credit of the country abroad, and for the expulsion of all the gold coins from the currency at Home. Instead of the currency including the two legal tenders which Congress was ignorantly attempting to secure, it would consist of one only, and that the one least worthy of the nation's greatness. Such were the theories of those who "prophesied before they knew!" And now for the facts which have become historical! Since the passing of the Bland Act ten years since, the United States has added to its legal tender metallic currency more than 130 millions sterling of gold—*an amount 12 per cent. greater than all that Great Britain now has*—and less than fifty-one millions sterling in silver. While coining two standard dollars the country was attracting five gold dollars! Never did facts more decisively antagonize the Law of the Prophets; neve was the common sense of the nation more completely vindicated! So much for the fine-spun theories of those who undertook to show that coinage at a ratio of 1 to 16 would drive out gold; that Congress had undertaken to make water run up-hill; that, in short, they, the critics, were vastly superior people, while, as Carlyle once said of his surroundings, the remainder were "fifty millions, mostly fools!" Ignorant people may still be found who, seeing some thousands of tons of these dollars piled up in the Treasury vaults at Washington, are asking for what purpose they were coined. The fact that three-fourths of these coins are in active circulation in the form of silver certificates—paper notes —and the fact that no American will burden his pockets with metallic currency, whether of gold or silver, will account for these hoards in the reserve. There is to-day more gold coin in the Treasury than silver: some 190 millions of gold dollars as compared with 180 millions silver. But when it was found that critical essays of the superior persons as to the absurdity of the Bland legislation could make no head at all, and that the "folly theory" had no effect upon the phalanx of "Silver men," who, while two-thirds strong in Congress, were in the constituencies themselves about as the coinage ratio, 16 to 1, then there commenced an attack upon Congress by many of the leading papers in England— papers, too, of the very highest standing—for which probably no parallel can be found in the entire history of journalism. For, indeed, it was left to a handful of leader-writers to point out, not for a week or two, but by a sustained attack that lasted for years, that, if not fools, the Silver men at Washington were a compact band of rogues, who had sold their consciences and their constituents for the silver dollars of the Rocky Mountain miners. That, in short, two-thirds of both Houses, because they refused to join in a crusade against silver, which crusade President Grant declared had originated in a fraud on Congress in 1873, and because they refused further to take the view that "dear money," showing its effects in rapidly falling prices, was a blessing in disguise, and that it was the first business of Congress by contracting the currency of the country to make the rich man richer by making the poor man poorer—because the majority had given a legitimate expression in Congress to views contrary to these, that therefore this majority was composed either of the owners of silver mines or of men who were in the pay of some Lobby subsidized by the Comstock "Bonanza." Here was a Bill, intended by supplying some coinage demand for silver to support the price of that metal, and a Bill, the continuance of which was declared by Mr. Goschen a little later to be of vital importance to the industries of Lancashire, and which is to-day determining the profit and the future of England's trade with the myriad-peopled East, and yet we were gravely assured in the English Press that it was a Bill corruptly devised in the interests of a few scattered mining camps in Colorado and Nevada! Incredible as such charges were, it is still more incredible that they should have made a profound and lasting impression on public opinion in England, an impression even to-day not wholly effaced. The value of the annual output of silver in the United States is some ten millions sterling; the value of the annual production of hens' eggs is some sixteen millions sterling. We shall next be told that Congress is in the pay of the hen-wives of the Republic, because it refuses to forbid the consumption of hens' eggs!

The Bland Bill is not a complete Bill. Quite true. But judged by its results it was a valuable and a careful measure intended to tide the world over a crisis. There may be different opinions as to its breadth and sufficiency. But no intelligent observer will question that by taking a portion of the loose silver off the market, it has availed to steady the fall of silver that was inevitable from unwise and ill-considered legislation, which fall and the fall of all prices with it must otherwise have been on such a scale that an unparalleled monetary crisis would doubtless have occurred.

III.

THE HISTORY OF PRICES

HAVING drawn attention, in the earlier of the two preceding chapters, to the successful attempt made in the Legislatures of Europe to "scale down" all prices by forcing up the value of gold, and in the second chapter to a similar attempt which, after being all but successful, was detected and defeated in America—and having in both endeavoured to show why this so-called "silver question" is destined to become, a little later in the Eastern hemisphere, as to-day in the Western, a leading political issue—let me now pass on to make a short survey of the world's history of prices, and of their fluctuations. Of course it is neither possible nor necessary to examine the fluctuations that may have occurred over short periods: my intention is merely to show that the general range of prices has been largely controlled by the increase in, or the diminution of, the output of the money metals from the mines. That when from the earliest times in the world's history population and production have increased more rapidly than the stock of currency, then prices have fallen, the relations between creditor and debtor have become strained, and great social troubles have resulted. That such effects should have followed such causes will not appear surprising, even after a casual examination. At the outset I wish to disclaim any intention of attaching too exclusive an importance to the "quantity theory" of money, in raising or depressing prices. At the present time, no doubt, there are other agencies at work, such as improved machinery, the development of electricity and steam, which, notwithstanding that prodigious increase in population of which they have been the parent, would account probably for a portion of the recent fall of prices. But it must not be forgotten that industrial developments have been going steadily forward from the earliest history of civilization, and yet prices have not been falling, but, on the contrary, perpetually rising. Indeed, it is not too much to affirm, that the rise of prices has, during a period of two thousand years, been an efficient indicator of the comparative progress of civilization. When prices have fallen for a time, then we recognize reaction—the ebb of the tide ; while the steadier the rise of prices—metallic prices—the greater has ever been the stimulus to industry, to enterprise, and to the accumulation of capital.

The historian Alison has very happily expressed the universality of the monetary influence. He writes :—

The two greatest events that have occurred in the history of mankind have been directly brought about by a successive contraction and expansion of the circulating medium of society. The fall of the Roman Empire, so long ascribed, in ignorance, to slavery, heathenism, and moral corruption, was in reality brought about by a decline in the silver and gold mines of Spain and Greece. And, as if Providence had intended to reveal in the clearest manner the influence of this mighty agent on human affairs, the resurrection of mankind from the ruin which those causes had produced was owing to a directly opposite set of agencies being put in operation. Columbus led the way in the career of renovation ; when he spread his sails across the Atlantic he bore mankind and its fortunes in his barque. The annual supply of the precious metals for the use of the globe was tripled ; before a century had expired the prices of every species of produce were quadrupled. The weight of debt and taxes insensibly wore off under the influence of that prodigious increase. In the renovation of industry the relations of society were changed, the weight of feudalism cast off, the rights of man established. Among the many concurring causes which conspired to bring about this mighty consummation, the most important, though hitherto the least observed, was the discovery of Mexico and Peru. If the circulating medium of the globe had remained stationary, or declining, as it was from 1815 to 1849, from the effects of the South American revolution and from English legislation, the necessary result must have been that it would have become altogether inadequate to the wants of man; and not only would industry have been everywhere cramped, but the price of produce would have universally and constantly fallen. Money would have every day become more valuable: all other articles measured in money less so; debt and taxes would have been constantly increasing in weight and oppression. The fate which crushed Rome in ancient, and has all but crushed Great Britain in modern, times, would have been that of the whole family of mankind. All these evils have been entirely obviated, and the opposite set of blessings introduced, by the opening of the great treasures of Nature in California and

Australia. Before half a century has elapsed, the price of every article will be tripled, enterprise proportionally encouraged, industry vivified, debts and taxes lessened.

If these bright anticipations have been disappointed, and if in Europe we are to-day again confronted by those social troubles from which we escaped so providentially in the middle of this century, the reaction has resulted in a very large measure from the betrayal of silver by the legislatures of the West. In full view of the beneficial results of " cheap money " from the mines, in full view of the glorious effects of 600 million sterling of gold added rapidly to the world's stocks, the attempt has yet been made during the lifetime of that very generation which was a witness of this universal prosperity, to strike down silver, to lop off nearly one-half of the active currency of the world. Instead, therefore, of the blessing of a full and expanding currency and of enterprise stimulated by rising prices, the currency has been deliberately starved, a money famine has been contrived, so that, while prices have everywhere fallen, the burden of all debt is doubled. Here is again " the winter of our discontent."

At the close of the 15th Century, when

America was discovered, it is estimated that the monetary stock of Europe did not exceed forty millions sterling, while the annual produce of the mines was less than £100,000. At that time the average price of wheat in England was twelve shillings, and the price of a good bullock thirty shillings, while, as compared with the range of prices to-day, all other commodities were similarly " cheap." Then what is known as the " Silver Age " in the world's history commenced with the discovery of silver mines in America. In 1545 the immense veins of Potosi were opened, and as the annual supply rose to two millions sterling—to twenty times the yield at the commencement of the century—so also before the close of the 16th Century, while the monetary stock of Europe had increased sixfold, all prices were found to have quadrupled. From this time, although the yield of the mines continued to increase steadily, so that in the early years of this century the annual addition was nearly ten millions sterling, yet so large and extending was the area of distribution, and so immense the increase both of production and population, that from 1650 to 1800 a fair level only of prices was maintained.

To come now to the currency history of our

own century. Mr. Jacob, the historian of the precious metals, in his great work published in 1831, showed that the monetary stock of Europe and America had decreased between 1809 and 1830, owing to losses, abrasion, and the requirements of the Arts, from 380 millions to 313 millions; and when, considering the natural tendency of this contraction to lower the scale of all prices, he writes: "If the prices of commodities were regulated solely by the quantity of the circulating medium, there would have been a fall of 13 per cent. from this cause in these twenty years, and of 32 per cent. from the increase of population in Europe and America, causing a natural decline of prices at the rate 42 per cent." But, owing to the disturbing effect of issues of inconvertible paper money, and also to the difficulty of averaging prices in the days before railroads, when prices low in one locality were often at famine rates a hundred miles away, Mr. Jacob was unable to establish that there had been any such fall as the figures of the monetary stock appeared to suggest, and he says, therefore:—" Owing to circumstances, whose influence it is difficult to calculate, the depression of prices which would be the natural result of a diminution of money, and an increase of population and exchangeable goods, has been either prevented or lessened."

But the later investigations made by Mr. Newmarch, and confirmed by the painstaking ability of Professor Jevons, show that the fall of prices which Jacob only recognizes as *theoretically* probable, but which he failed to detect, had actually taken place, and was on an even greater scale than the monetary figures indicated. Jevons has established that between 1809 and 1833, prices fell 43 per cent.; while between 1809 and 1849 prices had fallen "in the ratio of 100 to 41."

This is very interesting. Jacob admitted the theory and drew attention to it, even when the result appeared refractory; while to-day, although we have to guide us the fact of a currency contraction in metallic currency countries, and also the fact of a huge fall of prices, we are yet asked by a number of ingenious persons who run about looking for sun-spot theories or for surplus stocks which have no existence, to warm their mares' nests, and reject the experience of the past! In the 15th Century the price of a quarter of wheat, now thirty shillings, was only twelve shillings; the implements of agriculture, at that time most rude and imperfect, have ever since been improving. If prices are to fall with improvements in machinery and distribution, wheat then at ten shillings should be to-day at two shillings per quarter. And this equally disposes of the "overproduction" argument so frequently advanced to account for low prices. There was no over-production of wheat in the 15th Century; on the contrary, half the world was periodically in danger of starving. Wheat was at twelve shillings then, as compared with thirty to-day, and this clearly because money was then much scarcer than now, and its purchase power therefore proportionally greater. Those who abuse that hapless adjective "cheap," and who tell us that the fall of all prices is beneficial because it cheapens bread, would doubtless also tell us that the two-penny loaf of the 15th Century was "cheaper" than the four-penny loaf to-day. And to minds of that order the present contraction of the world's currency at the hands of the Legislatures, and the consequent wild tumble of prices, appears no doubt to be an effort of modern scientific statesmanship nearly equivalent to the finding of the philosopher's stone. History, however, will be likely to agree that such currency tinkering, which at the expense of the general community has built up most of the great fortunes of the century, stands in much the same relation to statesmanship that picking pockets does to philanthropy.

Those years of maximum "cheapness" between 1830 and 1850 were marked by the extraordinary sufferings of all classes of the community. The distress occasioned by the continuous fall of prices is reflected in these words, which, in 1832, Disraeli addressed to his constituents: "*Ireland in rebellion; the farmer in doubt; the shipowner in despair; our merchants without trade; the revenue declining; the wealthy hoarding their useless capital.*" To this position then, as to-day, the country had been brought by a contraction of the currency. From this crisis the world was only rescued in 1849 by the discovery of the great treasure-trove of the American Continent, which three years later was to be supplemented by the larger supplies still from the river-beds of Australia. Here was the commencement of the golden age in the world's history—the age of gold, "cheap," because abundant; the age of universal enterprise; the age of high rates of interest, because of the stimulus afforded to investment from the knowledge that prices were rising. Taking 100 as the index number, denoting the average of prices in 1850, Soetbeer estimates that the index number for 1870 was 125; Jevons, 121; the *Economist's* table prepared, I believe, by the late Mr. Walter Bagehot, 140. Were those years of rapidly advancing prices, years memorable also for a prosperity widespread and even universal? Happily, the answer to this question can be received direct from those who lived in that sunshine. What wonderful years those were for all classes! Wealth increased; wages advanced; each class of the community recognized its promotion to a higher plane of comfort, of leisure, and education; bread and meat were becoming "dearer;" but were they ever before or since *so really cheap*.

The annual addition to our gold currency during those years averaged more than $4\frac{1}{2}$ millions; so that, in 1878, according to M. de Laveleye's estimate we had 145 million sovereigns in our currency. Six years later Mr. Fremantle, the Director of the Mint, estimated the amount at less than 121 millions; and now the official report just issued by Mr. Kimball, the Director of the United States Mint, states that there has been yet a further reduction of twenty millions sterling! If these figures are even approximately correct, we have lost nearly thirty per cent. of our entire legal tender currency *in less than ten years!* What wonder under such conditions that since the "outlawry of silver" by Germany in 1873, prices have been falling "by leaps and bounds." The evidence given before Lord Iddesleigh's Trade Commission all pointed in the same direction: no traders knew where they stood; goods were losing their value, while on the shelf of the warehouse, and having been consigned to some market across the ocean, the tidings of a fresh fall was sure to meet them on arrival! Every witness spoke of the fall of prices, and the disaster consequent upon the fall. In one trade it was a fall of 20 per cent., in another of fifty. The crisis, all agreed, was a price crisis; demand was increasing; supplies seemed to be diminishing; and yet prices were all the time going steadily downwards.

Mr. Sauerbeck, whose tables of prices are now regularly published by the Statistical Society, and who occupies in this connection much the same position to-day that was formerly filled by Professor Jevons, has taken as his index number 100, to denote the average of prices between 1867 and 1877. The margin of variation is quite extraordinary. In 1873, the 100 had risen to 111, while in 1878 it had fallen to 87. In 1879 it was 83, and in the succeeding years it was 88, then 85, then 84, then 82, then 76, then 72. In 1886 it had fallen to 69, while for the month of September 1887 it was 68·7 ! The average of prices for the principal articles, writes Mr. Sauerbeck, for the first nine months of the year 1887 is the lowest recorded for a hundred years. With the exception of somewhat higher prices for tin, and lately for Manila hemp, there is only one article which has experienced a considerable rise, viz., coffee, on account of the failure of the Brazil crop. English wheat was in September last 47 per cent. below the average point, the lowest point touched since 1761. Sugar is now 50 per cent., tea 48 per cent., pig iron 41 per cent., copper 47 per cent., coals 30 per cent., cotton 45 per cent., merino wool 33 per cent., meat and butter 15 per cent., below the average of 1867-1877; while tin is at par and coffee 21 per cent. higher.

Is the world with some £5,000,000,000 sterling of national debt, the interest payable in gold, returning to the prices current in the 15th century?

IV.

THE FALL OF PRICES.

UNDER the above title two articles have recently appeared from the pen of Mr. David A. Wells, in the *Contemporary Review*. The desire of the writer is to demonstrate that the fall of prices, where it has occurred, is the result of such natural causes as increased supplies, improved machinery and lower freight charges. The stock arguments of Messrs. Mulhall and Fowler are again made the most of, and although, as I pointed out in a previous chapter, the course of prices has, for hundreds of years past, been rising *pari passu* with increased production and the developments of science, although between 1850 and 1875, years by comparison with the previous quarter of the century characterized by the universal development of science, prices rose some 40 per cent., still Mr. Wells invites us, with a sweet reasonableness, to abandon once and for all the currency theory of the fall of prices, in favour of his statement of "supply and demand." If I enter upon an extended examination of these papers, I do so in no spirit of hostility to Mr. Wells, but only because he ably represents a certain school of writers who are always getting in the way of the demands for currency reform. As for Mr. Wells himself, any argument he advances is entitled to respectful consideration. He is a statistician of accepted position, and he is also the leader in the United States of a Salvation Army which makes up for any deficiency in its numbers by its unwearied enthusiasm in spreading the gospels of the Cobden Club. But the line of argument taken by Mr. Wells in the pages of the *Contemporary Review*, while peculiar to himself and a diminishing number of disciples, is, it seems to me, no answer whatsoever to our assertion that the present contraction of the world's currency, and further, and more important still, the dislocation of the old "par of exchange" between the two metals, must inevitably be followed by a corresponding fall of prices in gold countries. Such is the position we take; but the moment we invite discussion, Mr. Wells very adroitly leads us off into a very labyrinth of statistics, which are meant to show that the fall of prices has followed from the activity of the inventor! If to save trouble we at once admit every point claimed by Mr. Wells, as to increased production and diminished freight charges, still all this merely emphasizes the prodigious importance of the reply to what is an entirely distinct question—" Are not the currency conditions, and our knowledge of what has happened in past times from similar conditions, such as to enable us to forecast a fall of some forty per cent. in prices?" If it is a fact that the conditions of supply and demand account of themselves for a fall of forty per cent., how enormously this increases the urgent nature of our claim for currency reform! If the tendency to a fall of forty per cent. in prices, because of the reasons advanced by Mr. Wells, had yet been more than counteracted by an immense *increase* in the production of the precious metals, then that Legislation which has deprived silver of its legal tender prerogative, would appear less unreasonable; but Mr. Wells' attitude is that of a doctor whose remedy for one broken leg is the fracture of the other! We have had a general fall of forty per cent. in prices; the currency conditions would of themselves account for such a fall; still we are assured by Mr. Wells that the entire fall is to be accounted for on other and entirely distinct grounds—very well then, it is clear that a further fall, more perilous and more disastrous, still awaits us, unless something is done to counteract the insidious agencies at work. Mr. Wells, and those who think with him, have unconsciously done us the very greatest service. Clearly if prices are collapsing from natural causes also, it is high time to call public attention to the suspicious doings of the Legislatures, in running amuck at silver. But while gratefully admitting the figures of production and of freights which Mr. Wells adduces to support his views, it is quite clear that his great mastery of statistics deserts him completely in his investigation of the Currency Question itself. The confusion of ideas resulting from mixing up the stock of *currency* with the money market stock of *loanable capital* is apparent in almost every page of the second article. For example, Mr. Wells writes (p. 633): "But the years from 1875 to 1879 inclusive, *taking the English market* as the criterion, were characterized generally by an excessive supply of money and currency of all kinds: and the same has been true of the period from 1880 to 1886-87, when if the *supply of money from gold was constantly diminishing, contrary results would seem to have been inevitable.*" But surely Mr. Wells must admit that, if owing to currency contraction or any other cause, prices are falling, there will always be an excessive supply of money seeking investment at the money centres. The supply of money may have diminished, but in the face of falling prices the demand for it will naturally have diminished faster still. There is all the difference in the world between *buying* gold and *borrowing* gold. It is when prices are rising that the loan demand for money is active; rising prices stimulate borrowing and investment, and are therefore always followed by a rising bank rate. M. de Laveleye writes of the money crisis caused in Hamburg in 1820 by the fall of prices that "the premium on gold mounted up to ten per cent., while the rate of interest remained extremely low, discount falling to only $1\frac{1}{2}$ per cent., a proof of the extreme stagnation of business."

Mr. Wells advertises very usefully the estimate made by M. Soetbeer and Mr. Pixley of the average yearly amount of gold available since 1850 *for the supply of coin.* Of course any such estimate must be largely speculative, but Mr. Wells makes the really extraordinary error of supposing that these estimates are estimates of the total additional *supply* from the mines. He writes (p. 636) :—

That the world's annual product of gold consequent upon the exhaustion of the mines in California and Australia has largely diminished in recent years, is not disputed. *Opinions as to the extent of this reduction of supply* are, however, widely at variance. *This is illustrated* by the following tables, presented in the "First Report of the British Commission on the recent changes in the relative values of the precious metals," which give the estimates of Messrs. Soetbeer of Germany and Pixley of London, two of the best recognized authorities on this subject, as to the average yearly amount of gold available for the supply of coin at different periods since 1850:—

Soetbeer.	Pixley.
1857-60 ... £22,780,000	1852-60 ... £27,600,000
1861-70 ... £14,060,000	1861-70 ... £17,600,000
1871-80 ... £10,255,000	1871-80 ... £18,700,000
1881-84 ... £ 3,050,000	1881-85 ... £11,200,000

But these are estimates, not of gold produced, but merely of the balance probably remaining over after the requirements for the arts and manufactures have been satisfied. M. Soetbeer has evidently classed as gold "*absorbed*," the several millions which are annually drained away to be hoarded in British India, while Messrs. Pixley and Abel have classed these millions as still *available* for currency purposes, the apparent discrepancy in the estimates is therefore largely accounted for. The great danger of statistics is in this: the public can be relied upon to add two and two together for themselves, but if pelted with paper millions, any statement is accepted, and every one who for a few years writes in millions, no matter how inexactly, becomes "an authority." Recently in the House of Commons Mr. Gladstone quoted some figures of Irish evictions on the authority of an Irishman, Mr. Michael Mulhall—Mr. Balfour challenged the figures which were established to be inaccurate in the ratio of 1 to 5! Now, Mr. Wells quotes the same authority as stating that in

Great Britain the ratio of metallic money used to the whole commerce of the country is only 20 per cent., the ratio rises in Germany to 34 per cent., in the United States to 58 per cent.; and in France to 85 per cent. Furthermore the banking facilities of the world, according to the same authority, have increased since 1840 eleven-fold or three times greater than the increase of commerce and thirty times greater than that of population.

It is really impossible to accept such figures as these as requiring serious analysis. What is the commerce of a country? The annual production

of wealth in the United States is upwards
of two thousand millions sterling, its *commerce*,
as this wealth on its way from the producer to
the consumer changes hands many times, is many
times greater; but if we accept this ratio of
metallic money not to commerce but even to
produced wealth, then, according to Mr. Mulhall,
or at least to his commentator, the United States
must have nearly twelve hundred millions sterling
of metallic money, whereas, according to the last
report of the Director of the United States Mint,
the amount is not much more than half as many
dollars. But if the figures here quoted are
intended to suggest that cash transactions in the
United States as between buyer and seller are
nearly three times as frequent as in England—
that is in the ratio of 58 to 20—this statement
seems to me to be also wildly inaccurate. I
believe, on the contrary, that in no country in the
world is business conducted to so dangerous an
extent, on a basis of credit, as it is in the United
States. The Americans are even more than
ourselves a commercial nation, a "Nation of
Shopkeepers;" the entire volume of their commerce is doubtless as much greater than that of
Great Britain as their population is greater than
that of Great Britain; so that if in the United

States three exchanges were effected by means of metallic money as compared with one in England, the volume of metallic money *per capita* would require to be greater in the United States than in England, whereas it is slightly less—is, according to the last report of the Director of the United States Mint, sixteen dollars and forty-nine cents, as compared with sixteen dollars and fifty-two cents in England.

Whether, as Mr. Mulhall goes on to remark, the banking facilities of the world have increased "eleven-fold since 1840" is merely guesswork; but, in any case, to attempt to argue as to monetary requirements from the ratio of banking facilities to the world's population, is as ridiculous as to try to establish a ratio between professional beauty and the Rocky Mountains! There is in either case no common denominator. If a complete banking system could be established to-morrow in China, this, so far from diminishing the currency requirements of the world, would, by extending the metallic area, enormously increase those requirements—would have a similar effect in redistributing silver money as the action of Germany had in 1873 on the gold stocks of the world. China would require perhaps two hundred millions sterling of currency, and subject

to such a demand for silver—the ratio of 1 to
15½ would be restored at one jump.[1] That credit

[1] The *North China Herald*, published at Shanghai, questions this view in a very interesting editorial of March 23rd. "Now, everybody who knows China knows that this country possesses a very complete banking system, so far as the number of banks and their extension all over the Empire goes. It is not the best banking system in the world, and it would bear improvement and modernizing to a very great extent. Except, perhaps, Scotland, China is more amply banked than any other country that we know of. What is wanted, to enable the officials and the mercantile classes to improve their financial methods, is the formation of a National Bank, which shall have branches in the large cities, transacting ordinary banking business and assisting the Government as national banks in other countries assist theirs. But though a part of the capital of such a bank would require to be imported, in some form or other, if foreigners were allowed to hold shares in it, it is by no means certain that any large amount would require to be provided in this way. And it is highly improbable that a sum anything like two hundred millions sterling would be necessary to provide a currency. China possesses and always has possessed a large amount of sycee silver, and if the Government determined to issue a coinage much of that silver would be used for the purpose. Probably the best policy for the Government to adopt would be to offer some advantages to the owners of sycee to send it to the mints to be coined. Sycee would go out of currency as soon as a coinage was made, as we presume it would be made, the only legal tender, and the mercantile classes, at all events, would get rid of their silver as soon as possible. It is by no means the first time that we have seen bi-metallists, and some who are not bi-metallists, express their belief that China would, as soon as she determined to issue a coinage,

has not taken the place of metallic money, Mr. Giffen also agrees. He writes: "I much doubt whether any serious economy has been effected with regard to exchanges accomplished by the substitution of credit for gold." The Clearing

or commence to construct railways on a large scale, require a great amount of silver. Many newspapers hailed with great satisfaction the Concessions to the American bankers last year, because they took it for granted that a large quantity of silver would be required to carry out the schemes. So far from that being the case, every ton of rails or each locomotive that was imported would make China a buyer of gold, or bills of exchange, to pay for them. Anything which increases the debt of China to the West tends to place her finances—as far as these refer to the outside world—in the same position as the finances of India, for the more payments she has to make to Europe or America the greater the amount of gold exchange she will require to remit. Of course a considerable or even a large part of the first cost of railways, and perhaps of other public works, might be raised in loans abroad, but even so that would not lead to the import of any large amount of silver. It is not known how much silver comes to and is sent away from Hongkong and China, but persons acquainted with the trade are of opinion that as much is exported as is imported. And a considerable part of what comes from San Francisco is sent to pay drafts which the banks in that city issue on Hongkong to returning Chinese or to Chinese merchants. The supply of sycee seems sufficient for the trade of the country, supplemented as it is by copper *cash* and by gold and bankers' drafts as remittances. But no believer in China taking off a large quantity of silver, for imperial purposes, has ever, so far as we know, shown what she could give in exchange, supposing she required the metal."

House returns in London show also of late years no expansion, but on the contrary a steady diminution.

But the most extravagant misstatement of all is to be credited to Mr. Wells himself. After alleging that every addition to the stock of gold and silver is an addition "to the fund available for exchanges" (a statement so inexact as to require no comment beyond the remark, that a gold plate is no more available to effect exchanges than when its gold was yet in the bowels of the earth), Mr. Wells proceeds to say (p. 639):

The aggregate sum by which the yearly average amount of gold available for coinage fell off during the period from 1861-70, as compared with that from 1852-60, when the mines of California and Australia were most productive, was, adopting Mr. Pixley's estimates, less than one hundred millions sterling, a sum absolutely great, but most inconsiderable—less than *one-sixth of* 1 *per cent.*—in comparison with the amount of gold believed to have been in existence in civilized countries in 1885.

Now, apart from the fact that this "most inconsiderable" sum is about equal to the entire gold in currency to-day in Great Britain, what is that sum of which a hundred millions represents less than one-sixth of one per cent.?—Why a sum of upwards of sixty thousand millions sterling! No estimate, however, is in existence which places the entire gold currency not of "civilized countries" but of the whole world at more than seven hundred and twenty millions, or the total of gold of whatever kind, at more than fourteen hundred and sixty millions. So that actually this "inconsiderable" deficiency, instead of being *one-sixth of one per cent.*, is about one-seventh of the whole! Of course Mr. Wells will be the first to admit the inaccurracy of his own figures. The error is one of mere carelessness, but none the less mistakes on such a scale from a writer of such mark, are most deplorable in dealing with such a subject. The people who read Mr. Wells' articles accept them as data available for fresh currency literature, and are just the people least likely to go to the trouble of reading these corrections,—people hostile to silver, hostile to monetary reform, and only anxious to absorb some figures, correct or incorrect, which they can reproduce when required, alleging the authority of Mr. David A. Wells.[1]

[1] For a review of Mr. Wells' figures of "over production," see Appendix A., republished from the *New York Commercial Chronicle.*

Mr. Wells' two articles, excellent in themselves and full of valuable material, are entirely deformed by his references to the currency subject, a subject which lies quite outside of the field of statistical study in which he has been such a patient worker. Himself the most honest of writers, he yet, from a mere want of perception, brings within the compass of five lines M. Cernuschi and Mr. Sauerbeck as making statements which leave upon the mind of the reader an impression exactly the opposite of that which those distinguished economists would wish to convey. M. Cernuschi had written to the *Economist* that "the fall of prices which is complained of, is not due to what has been called a scarcity of gold—a scarcity which is purely imaginary;" and this unguarded remark is quoted by Mr. Wells and has been quoted by a hundred others as evidence that there is gold enough *alone* to maintain prices. Every currency student would understand that M. Cernuschi was referring to the fall of prices as resulting, not from the scarcity of gold, but from the outlawry of silver, which before 1873 not only did a large portion of the work now done by gold, but which maintained also a steady "par of exchange" between the metals—a distinct question which I shall consider in a later chapter. If the Legislatures were suddenly to agree that vegetarianism was the right thing, and that man must live by bread alone, it is evident that a famine would occur. The citizen who previously required half a loaf, plus fish and meat and eggs, would now require in the absence of all other food two loaves; in one sense of the word there would be no scarcity of wheat: the world's wheat harvest might be the largest recorded. There would be no natural scarcity,—only an artificial, a *legislated* scarcity; and it was in this sense, and this only, that very unfortunately M. Cernuschi denied that there was a "scarcity of gold." Mr. Wells immediately after, with the same idea in his mind, quotes Mr. Sauerbeck as declaring that a "scarcity of gold as understood by bankers, does not exist," and this is quite true *as undersood by bankers;* the banks were never so full of idle unloanable capital, but to suggest that this is a sign of an abundant currency is absurd. There are a hundred million sovereigns in Great Britain; if these sovereigns were all known to be lying idle in the Bank of England, it would be a little bewildering to argue that *therefore* there were plenty of sovereigns in currency outside the Bank!

Nor I think is Mr. Wells luckier in his theory of diminished freight charges. Lower freights are less the *cause* than the *consequence* of low prices. If the material of which ships and railroads are built falls in price, owing to a currency contraction, freights will fall also. If a ship can be built for half the money, freights will fall accordingly: low freights are the results particularly of cheaper loanable capital, of cheaper material and cheaper labour, which are themselves all primary symptoms of a contracted currency. To say, therefore, that prices are low because freights are low, is merely to allege that prices are low because prices are low!

Finally, I would refer Mr. Wells, and those who think with him, to a paper of the late Mr. Stanley Jevons published in December 1869 in the *Journal of the Statistical Society*. He was replying to those who alleged the "supply and demand theory," as a reason for the then rapid *rise* of prices, and he was insisting that prices were rising because of a currency expansion, just as we to-day urge that prices are falling because of a currency which by comparison with those times has become contracted. Jevons, who was the most fair-minded and reasonable of all the advocates of so-called "monometallism," writes:

THE FALL OF PRICES.

To complete the argument I have only to ask those who think that the growth of population, the increase of demand, or the progress of trade is the cause of the rise in prices, whether population, demand, trade, &c., were not expanding before 1849, not so rapidly perhaps as since, but still expanding; and how it is that causes of the same kind have produced falling prices before 1849, and rising prices since? To gain some notion of the degree of probability of conclusions on this subject (the rise of all prices), it has occurred to me to apply the ordinary methods of the theory of probabilities to the results stated in my pamphlet on the value of gold. The list of commodities there given (including cotton) contained thirty-six different articles, of which twenty-nine were found to have risen in price in 1862, as compared with the average of the years 1845-50, while only seven had fallen in price. All the alterations of price (excluding the extreme rise in the case of cotton) lay between a fall of 26 per cent. and a rise of 67 per cent., but most of the alterations were of about 10 or 20 per cent. Regarding each of these thirty-six commodities as a separate and independent measure of the alteration in the value of gold, I first took the average rise of prices, namely, 16 per cent., as the most probable estimate which these thirty-six measures give, and then proceeded to calculate by the ordinary method of least squares the probable error of the results. . . . . It may be safely said that the odds are 10,000 to 1 in favour of a real depreciation of gold. The meaning of this is that the *chances are ten thousand to one against a series of disconnected and casual circumstances having caused the rise of price—one in the case of one commodity, another in the case of another—instead of some general cause acting over them all.* . . . . . The tables of your Annual Review unmistakably prove the existence of a rise; to what must we attribute it? To growth of population and trade? I think that the growth of population and trade tend to lower prices by increasing the use of gold, and to this cause we may reasonably attribute the fall of prices before 1849. But to attribute to the same cause, as some do, the diametrically opposite change which has occurred since 1849, is illogical in the extreme. The normal course of prices in the present progressive state of things is, I think, downwards, but for twenty years at least this normal course has been checked or even reversed, and why should we hesitate to attribute this abnormal effect to the contemporary and extraordinary discoveries of gold? It would not be difficult to show that not only have prices risen during the period in question, but that the relations of society have readjusted themselves in accordance. While statisticians have been disputing, society has practically accepted the fact of a rise. The pay of the army is increased; the whole of the Civil Service, and the staff of the Bank of England receive larger salaries, and could the information be obtained, I believe the same changes might be shown to have occurred in most private establishments.

Because of the depreciation of gold, consequent upon the great discoveries, wages and salaries were all raised. Now a more than equivalent appreciation has occurred, not because of the scarcity of the precious metals, but because of radical legislative changes, whether dishonest or merely capricious.

The question now asked of our statesman is this: Which will cause the less social disturbance, the immediate reduction of all wages and salaries, or, on the other hand, the reversal of certain legislation, which from the very first was under suspicion, but which is now directly challenged as dishonest? Surely there can be little doubt as to the nature of the reply!

V.

MR. DAVID A. WELLS ON "BIMETALLISM."

THE arguments as to the Fall of Prices advanced by Mr. Wells in the October number of the *Contemporary Review*, even when they fail to carry conviction, are in themselves valuable, and his statistics of production will be found by all students of prices most useful for purposes of reference. In the number for November, where Mr. Wells reviews the currency aspect of the fall, he blunders badly; but what is to be said of the concluding paper of his series, which appears labelled "Bimetallism" in the December number of the *Review?* Mr. Wells is at all times such an agreeable writer that the position of a candid critic is an ungracious one. Just as no one reads the *Hunting of the Snark* with less enjoyment because at the close he is still puzzled as to the scientific grouping of the genus "Snark," so in Mr. Wells's paper on bimetallism, even where the author is at fault from evident unfamiliarity with his subject, he still rarely fails to be interesting. But if we are seriously required to consider this paper as a survey of "Bimetallism," by a standard writer, then it helps to explain why, to use the writer's own words, "there is no other economic problem concerning which there is so little comprehension on the part of the general public." For there is really nothing in this paper "bimetallic" except its title; the relation of the title to the contents is the relation between the announcement often seen in largest type in the American papers: "Ten Thousand Dollars Reward," to the assurance which follows that "St. Jacob's Oil cures all sprains."

Mr. Wells has, I believe, held the very responsible position of Secretary to the Treasury in the United States. We are all of us indebted to him for his careful statistical researches, but with much respect it must be evident to those who have even skirted the fringe of the Currency question, that Mr. Wells is but an ill-equipped recruit in this conflict around the Standards. No one who is in the habit of thinking out currency problems could possibly have made so extravagant a mistake as to write about a hundred millions of gold being a sum "most inconsiderable," as "less than one-sixth of one per cent."

of our gold stocks. Every man to whom the Currency question is even interesting carries it always in his mind as a point of departure that, whether a little more or a little less, there are only seven hundred millions sterling of gold in all the currencies of the world, and that when dealing with one hundred millions, he is dealing with a seventh and not a six-hundredth part of the whole. The perusal of any book of Mr. Dana Horton's, indeed, any one of a hundred recent speeches in congress, would have protected a compatriot against inaccuracies such as these. At least the third paper, published in December, might have corrected the statistical errors contained in the previous numbers.

And if there is one argument that makes more strongly than all others for the free coinage and unlimited legal tender of the two metals—an argument admitted to be quite sound even by Jevons—it is this: that the inconveniences and dangers of sudden derangements of prices are immensely diminished by the unlimited coinage of the two metals. How enormous was the service rendered to the world by the automatic action of the bimetallism of the French mints in the years that succeeded the great gold discoveries. Had France at that time been either on a single silver, or on a single gold, basis, then such masses of gold as were pouring into the world's markets could not have failed to inflate prices in gold standard countries to a most disastrous degree. So that instead of prices rising steadily some 35 per cent., they would no doubt have doubled or even trebled by "leaps and bounds." Thanks solely to the compensatory action of her bimetallic system, France sat in the middle of the commercial world as the universal money-changer, and quietly and almost imperceptibly exchanged a hundred millions sterling of her legal tender silver, for an equal amount of the new gold. France, as Chevalier well expressed it, was the "parachute" which *broke the fall of gold.* Suppose there had been no country keeping open mint, where masses of gold could be exchanged against equal masses of silver, one of two evils must have ensued: either a dislocation of trade, and wild gambling in "exchange" between all silver standard and gold standard countries, pending an adjustment of all prices, or otherwise a succession of money panics, the ruin of the bond-holding classes and frantic appeals to the legislatures to make changes of standard from gold, at that time depreciating rapidly, to silver, then as now by comparison stable. Thus it was that only for the "parachute"—the beneficent operation of the French monetary system —the most serious inflation of prices must have taken place, and, what is far more important still, we should now be suffering from a resultant contraction of all prices, on a scale similar to the antecedent rise. Prices having trebled would have again fallen by two-thirds; and as when gold is cheapest, speculation is most brisk, properties of all kinds, bought twenty years since, subject to fixed gold mortgages, amounting perhaps to fifty per cent. of their then value, would long since have changed hands, leaving the proprietor, through no fault of his own—penniless, the mortgagee everywhere in sole possession. So alarmed was M. Chevalier at the magnitude of the coming *fall* he saw in the value of gold, that even though he recognized the "parachute" afforded by bimetallic coinage at the French mints, yet he urged the world to revert to a single silver standard. Acting upon his suggestions and in order to protect the creditor classes from the coming depreciation of gold, Holland and Belgium demonetized gold, while Russia forbade the export of silver. And what has Mr. Wells to say of this equilibriating action of bimetallic France, which at a most critical time, and in the face of a most unexampled increase in the stock of one metal, yet availed to maintain a steady ratio of 1 to $15\frac{1}{2}$ *all* the world over? He says of it that "*there was a well-recognized movement in France against silver and in favour of gold from* 1853 *to* 1865!" The natural, inevitable movement mint-ward of the more abundant metal, when admitted to legal tender coinage, which is one of the admitted results of bimetallism is thus referred to a moral movement in the public mind against silver! Does Mr. Wells for a moment doubt that if the French mints were to-day open to free coinage of silver, as they were before 1875, silver would come forward and the tendency would be for gold to flow away from France into gold monometallic countries? And would Mr. Wells describe this also as a "well-recognized movement in France *against gold* and in favour of silver!" A few lines later he pays the highest possible tribute to the steadiness of silver, and says that never "would an ounce of silver exchange for so much of sugar, wheat, wool, iron, copper, or of most other commodities as at present." Here is the admission that silver possesses the very attribute required in a standard of value, namely, comparative stability. Prices measured in gold have fallen forty per cent.;

prices measured in silver, perhaps ten per cent. Which then is the fairer standard of values for classes and masses alike—for every one, in short, except the universal "Gold Bug!" And having thus made clear to us that in dealing with silver we are dealing with a good standard metal, in the very same five lines Mr. Wells goes on to give "a rational explanation of the decline since 1873 in the value of silver." What decline? Surely a moment since we were assured that silver had risen in value? And so we have secured from Mr. Wells this distinct admission—that the decline in silver is solely a decline in the gold value of silver, but that its commodity value, its measuring value, has not declined; that in fact it is *gold which is appreciating, not silver which is depreciating!* And this brings us to the one further point I intend to make as against Mr. Wells,—the question of the connection between the price of wheat and the price of silver. Let us avoid misleading jargon about international trade being international barter, and suppose that we are purchasing wheat for export from a ryot in the Punjaub. What does this ryot want for his wheat? Clearly rupees. Does he care, I ask him, whether he gets one rupee per maund, or two rupees? Certainly he cares; if the value of the rupee he receives, to buy cottons at the Bombay mills, to buy a cow, to buy labour, does not diminish, he would be twice as well off, he says, with two rupees as with one. Very well: then I am able to tell him that President Cleveland and both Houses of Congress have at last been converted by Mr. Wells and his friends and the Bland Act has been repealed; the inducement to fraudulent coinage has now become so much greater, that in order to protect the morals of their citizens the United States have agreed to withdraw from currency and sell all their legal tender silver, and to make use in future of a single legal tender—gold; that fifty millions sterling of silver is forthwith to be flung upon the London market! What will be the effect on its price of this deluge of the white metal? Certainly the silver ounce will fall to thirty pence, probably much lower; that is, the rupee is to be reduced from its old value of nearly a tenth, to the twentieth part of a sovereign. Now the price paid for Indian wheat to-day in the London market is three half-sovereigns per quarter, therefore the ryot who is to-day getting 22 silver rupees, will get for the same amount of wheat and the same amount of gold— thirty rupees; are we to understand that this rise

of price will fail to bring more wheat land into
cultivation, and will fail to stimulate the wheat
export trade of India at the expense of the British
and the American farmer? Suppose that rupees
could be bought in London at the rate of 40
to the pound sterling, and still the rupee maintained in India its purchase power, would that
have no effect on the proportion of the wheat
trade of England from the Punjaub on the one
hand, from Dakota and Minnesota on the other?
The ryot who cares nothing for the theories of
economists, merely says, "I want 22 rupees for
a quarter of wheat; if I can buy 22 rupees for
a sovereign I can afford to sell my wheat in
London for a sovereign a quarter. Mr. Wells
himself allows that an ounce of silver exchanges
for as much of sugar, wheat, &c., &c., as ever it
did; he affirms repeatedly that while the price of
the silver ounce has been falling from sixty pence
to 44 pence, yet the rupee, with the "perversity"
Mr. Goschen recently stigmatized, maintains in
India its full purchase power. Having admitted
the premises both major and minor, he resists
the inevitable conclusion, and says in his second
paper: "No one has been able to trace with any
degree of clearness any connection between the
two facts—between the fact of the fall in the

price of wheat and the fall in the price of silver." In his third paper also Mr. Wells writes: "Nothing is easier than to get into a state of mental confusion in respect to this matter." The "mental confusion" amounts to this: either there is a connection between the price of wheat and the price of silver, or Mr. Wells must be prepared to affirm that if the value of gold in the United States to buy every other commodity did not diminish, it would still be a matter of indifference to the Minnesota farmer whether he receives one dollar a bushel, or one hundred dollars a bushel, for his wheat![1]

[1] Replying to the questions of the Currency Commissioners, M. Cernuschi says of the "stimulus to exports from silver countries"—

"So long as exclusively Oriental articles such as tea and indigo were concerned, the fall of prices could displease nobody. Not so if articles are concerned which we ourselves produce—wheat, oilseed, and the like.

"I will speak only of the most important article, wheat.

"Many persons maintain that if Indian wheat be sold cheap, it is because it is produced cheap, because it is carried cheap to the shipping port, and because freights have considerably fallen. Were this the case the classical country of free trade might have no right to complain. But it is not so.

"To reckon the price of Indian wheat sold in England, there is no need to know what the production of that wheat costs, nor what the carriage to the shipping port costs. It is enough to know the price at which that wheat can be

F

It appears possible, however, that from the mistakes of Mr. David A. Wells, Mr. Mulhall, and other statisticians, when dealing with this subject, the world may arrive at a general conclusion of great importance. The science of statistics is clearly an inductive science—it is an adding together of units, dozens, and hundreds, to arrive at sums total. But economic science on

sold in England, and what has been laid out in maritime transport and sale expenses.

"Let us take the price of 33s. per quarter. Maritime transport and sale expenses are known to require an outlay of 6s. per quarter. Subtracting 6 from 33, there remain 27s., which at the exchange of 18d. produces 18 rupees. It follows that Indian wheat can be bought at 18 rupees on ship at Bombay, to be sold at 33s. in England. But to make these 18 rupees, if the bimetallic par at 2s. per rupee still existed, 36s. would be required instead of 27s. Difference 9s., which would have to increase the selling price if the bimetallic par had not disappeared.

"Indian wheat selling cheap, English wheat correspondingly falls. English agriculturists are forced to sell their wheat 9s. cheaper.

"This bounty by exchange has had the effect of stimulating wheat-growing in India, so that her exports of wheat have risen from 637,000 cwt. in 1872, to 21,000,000 cwt. in 1886,—an increase about as 1 to 33. Considering that the new arrivals of wheat are themselves by their magnitude the cause of a fall, a cause which would not exist if the bounty by exchange did not itself exist, it may be affirmed that English wheat would now be selling at 44s. to 47s. if the bimetallic par had not disappeared."

the other hand is an analytical science. Take this very subject of the Currency, and what is the method we employ in helping ourselves forward to conclusions? We take the history of the world, and we observe that during certain periods before and since the fall of the Roman Empire, there were periods of a flowing prosperity; and there were on the contrary periods of reaction; we make allowance for disastrous wars, for scientific and geographical discoveries, for the expansion of people, of trade, and of credit; we compare the output of the mines and the progress of nations from barbaric conditions of mere barter to their age of civilization—manifested among other things by their acceptance of a metallic currency. And we are able, as we believe, to establish a connection, almost self-evident, between the variation of prices and the variations in the local distribution of the money metals. And if this is so, we have also arrived at this point,—that statistics require an inductive method of mind, but currency investigation a deductive method; that as a general statement it may be accepted that the more eminent the statistician, the less he is qualified to guide us to reasonable conclusions in political economy. Of course I am not to be understood as affirming that this conclusion is an exact scientific truth: there are some "ambidexterous" minds which can keep reversing their methods of thought without any loss of power—can, so to speak, regulate their mental exchanges by a certain bimetallic receptiveness! Mr. Goschen I believe to be such an one, and in a lesser degree Mr. Giffen. The latter as a statistician has probably no living equal; but that he is also in touch with the currency problem, even those who disagree with his views will still be prepared to admit.

As a general statement, however, it holds good that there is no more *necessary* connection between the industry that enables a man to *collect* figures, and his efficient employment of these figures in the process of abstract reasoning, than there is between the genius of a Krupp or Armstrong, and the genius of a Turenne or a Wellington.

There is much more danger in extravagant reliance on statistics than is at all generally recognized. A high authority has made the discovery that political economy has been banished to Saturn; and beyond all doubt there is a revolt to-day all over the world, which is changing the face of politics, and which is adding immensely to the cohorts of the Socialists. The revolt indeed may almost be described as itself Socialism. And this is probably to be attributed not to any fallacies to be discerned in Economic Science, but to the nimbleness and the excesses of certain statistical professors. A man who describes himself as a Doctor, and who physics his fellow-citizens without the certificate of a diploma, probably will fetch up in jail; but upon the accuracy of generally-received statistics may, and often does, depend the direction of legislation in the State, and there should therefore be some penalty imposed upon figure vendors, whose variations from admitted facts exceed a fair margin.

VI.

NATIONAL DEBTS AND THE GROWTH OF SOCIALISM.

IN an article in the *Nineteenth Century* for October 1885 I drew attention in some detail to the aggravation of the burden of national debts, which may result from a fall of prices. What is a national debt? Clearly, although expressed in sovereigns or dollars or rupees, it represents a subscription of a certain portion of the capital of the community which, when converted into money, is paid into the coffers of the State. The iron-master realizes so many tons of iron; the cotton-spinner so much cotton; the farmer so many bullocks. Now if there was no such thing as money in the world, clearly where an iron-master lent the State one ton of iron, the State in returning the loan would have no possible right to tax the community by repaying two tons. Nor would the State stand excused on any such ground as that the cost of producing iron had meanwhile fallen. And yet this is exactly what the State is to-day doing all the world over! If

I am right in concluding that the contracted condition of the currencies, resulting from legislation, first in England and later in Germany, accounts for a fall of forty per cent. in prices, which fall from this cause has either already taken place or must inevitably occur a little later, then this fall of prices has added forty per cent. to the burden of our debt just as distinctly, just as directly, as though with prices steady, Governments had increased the number of sovereigns in those debts by 40 per cent., or had increased in that proportion the weight of the sovereign to enrich the bondholder at the expense of the community. Thus it happens that while Finance Ministers are economizing in hundreds, the debts themselves are growing at the rate of thousands!

It would be clearly quite impossible to express in terms of the produce represented by the sovereigns when borrowed, such a National Debt as that of Great Britain. The period during which it was contracted is a long one, and prices during that period have fluctuated between very wide limits. If it were possible, however, to make an exact statement of the National Debt in terms of the staple products of Great Britain, what a revelation it would appear of the enormous injustice done to the general community by the appreciation of gold.

During the second quarter of the year 1801, while consols had fallen to 54, the price of wheat was within nine pence of £8 per quarter. What is the meaning of consols at 54? It means that during the period of our history, when the debt was increasing most rapidly, Government was promising in return for £54 to repay at some future date £100, with interest in the mean time at 5 per cent., not on the £54 actually advanced, but on the £100 of nominal value. Now, suppose for a moment that at that time all prices were, as compared with prices to-day, as £8 the then price of wheat to thirty shillings the present price; and further that the 700 millions which we owe to-day had been all borrowed during that time—then clearly the same amount of debt which then represented a borrowing by the State of only ninety million quarters of wheat, is to-day represented by nearly 500 million quarters.

The national debt of the United States at the close of their war was more than 600 millions sterling, to-day it has been reduced to 230 millions, and yet so far from the debt itself being reduced, rather than the mere quotation of its amount in dollars, it would take more wheat or cotton, or iron or sugar, or maize—these are the staple products of the country—to redeem the third of the debt which remains now, than would have wiped out the entire debt at the scale of prices in which that debt was contracted. "But this is all very true," replies the bondholder and gold owner, "still at a time of crisis we showed such patriotic confidence in the future of the country that we deserve to get back four dollars where we lent one: It was a fair gamble and we were the winners." But as a matter of fact the money owner did nothing of the sort; the State commenced the deal by borrowing his money without his leave by the simple expedient of printing paper money wholesale, and making these notes legal tender. Every other property owner was taxed through an inflation of all prices equally with the bondholder. But he alone has been permitted to grow rich out of the misfortunes of his country. Alone of the community the State has bonused his patriotism: that bonus is neither more nor less than the difference in value between gold and greenbacks. The amount of the premium on gold has been the amount of the premium on this kind of patriotism!

And what classes of the community pay nine-tenths of all taxes? I believe that indirectly almost the entire sum of taxation is deducted from that share of production which is paid to labour. Mr. Edward Atkinson, of Boston, whose statistics may be accepted without hesitation, has estimated that the annual production of wealth in the United States amounts to ten thousand million dollars, of which sum, after providing for " domestic consumption "—the consumption on the farm or in the factory—9000 millions represent the product that comes to market; of this sum Mr. Atkinson finds that taxes consume 700 millions and the balance of 8300 millions is divided between capital and labour in the ratio of 1 to 10. If, therefore, there were no taxes at all, of the 700 millions absorbed by taxes, one-tenth would be taken by the capitalist, but nine-tenths by the workers. And if this conclusion holds good it is clear that the greater the fall of prices and the larger the share of production which must be converted into gold to be paid to bondholders, the longer must be the hours of labour. In short it is readily conceivable that gold debts might increase, not only relatively but absolutely—while prices fell to that point where the entire industrial production of a country was absorbed in the payments of interest to the owners of the National Debt. And bearing this possibility in mind, Lord Derby's recent speech at Liverpool is very significant. The national debts of Europe have risen from 400 millions at the commencement of the century to a present aggregate of nearly 5000 millions sterling. And Lord Derby, who is not an alarmist, warned his audience that the close of the century may probably witness an extensive repudiation of these increasing burdens. And because this can hardly be otherwise if prices are to fall further, such a forecast of the future by a leading statesman affords the best reply to those who say that as England is a creditor nation, and draws annually interest to the amount of eighty millions sterling from other countries, that therefore the greater the fall of prices the greater the amount of the produce of the foreigner which must be paid as annual tribute to England. This is true enough, but the question is how long will it be before debtor communities recognize that England was the first nation to sanction legislation intended to contract the currencies of the world, and thus to increase the burden of debt? And when this point has been made clear, and that in the form of "appreciated gold," the debts owing to

England have been already paid in full, both principal and interest, how long will it be before the example of partial repudiation set by Turkey comes to be extensively followed?

England has advanced some 2000 millions to various foreign countries on certain securities. The margin between the loan and the security diminishes day by day, with each fresh fall of prices. Surely he is a short-sighted creditor who fails to count the cost of such a condition of things if continued beyond a certain point! After the great gold discoveries in 1849 when from natural causes, by reason of *increased* supplies from the mines, gold was *depreciating* and the burden of the national debt *diminishing*, Jevons wrote of the effects of the new supplies: "The country may be said to be looking on, while every contract, including that of the national debt, is being violated against the intention of the contracting parties." To-day the same thing is occurring, and on a greater scale, not because of *natural causes*, but because of the direct interference of the Legislatures, in manipulating the currencies "*contrary to the intention of the contracting parties.*"

It is clear, therefore, that the developments of science in labour-saving machinery and in the process of a more economical distribution which should be every day diminishing the hours of labour, and increasing that share of production which is awarded to the working classes, has for ten years past, in consequence of the aggravation of all debt, been diverted so as to swell the fortunes of bondholders and bankers. The landowners, the owners of mills and mines, the owners of all that form of wealth which, being subject to the control of legislation, can be deprived of its rights, if the duties which follow from those rights are neglected—these classes are becoming impoverished by legislation, monetary legislation, framed so as to enrich the gold-owner, who is able from the nature of his wealth to evade his duties to the State and to remove his capital at a moment's notice to other investments in other lands.

To those who profess a convenient belief that although the fall of prices increases the burden of national debts, yet that a lessened cost of production avails to right the balance, I would recommend a short study of Egyptian finances to-day. There is a nation of peasant cultivators —six millions of people farming five millions of acres, whose agricultural implements are neither better nor worse than at the time when Joseph was sold by his brethren; nor is the tide of the same Nile which to-day brings to market the produce of the same fields in similar barges either faster or less fast, than five thousand years ago. Twenty-five years since Egypt was free of foreign debt, but in an evil hour, the ex-Khedive Ismail borrowed about a hundred millions sterling at enormous rates of interest in London and Paris. This money was not spent on internal improvements, but was squandered on the construction of twelve royal palaces in Cairo, and in the purchase of pictures and furniture for these palaces. The Levantine contractors who built the palaces made immense fortunes, and for the most part reinvested these fortunes in loans to the fellaheen at rates varying from two to six per cent. *per month!* Truly a vicious circle! The Khedive pledged the homesteads of his subjects to borrow money in London: this money passed on to foreign middlemen, who in turn lent it at usurious rates to the peasantry, who were themselves the security for the original loans! The cultivators were in the pleasant position of having to pay first seven per cent. to the foreign financier, and a further thirty per cent. per annum on the same money to the foreign contractor! To pay the interest on this

National Debt, each acre of cultivated land in Egypt has to convert enough of its produce into gold to send almost a sovereign yearly to the foreign creditor. In addition to this, each acre has to contribute a further share to the expenses of the home Government. The taxes of Upper Egypt are collected not in money, but directly in produce. The lower prices fall, the greater the amount of produce which is appropriated from each acre to pay the sovereign required of it. Since the time the debt was contracted the prices of the staple products of Egypt, cotton, sugar, wheat, and beans, have fallen more than 50 per cent. The Revenue for the current year shows a small surplus over the Budget Estimate, simply because cotton has risen nearly a penny per pound and sugar about three shillings a hundredweight. But if prices are to fall still further, the gold payments which Egypt owes to England, can only be exacted from a starving nation, by the most merciless exactions, and by the free use of the *kourbash*. Here is an instance, an extreme instance I admit, of that "appreciation of gold" about which philosophers with fixed incomes write so complacently, and which is said to be for the advantage of England the creditor nation.

Is the burden of judicial rents in Ireland, one half so grievous as the present burden of Egypt? And yet how different has been our treatment in the two countries of a disease absolutely identical!

Such is the nature of the disorder in Egypt, a country which owes one hundred millions of national debt out of the total of five thousand millions. And in other countries in Europe—in Russia, France, Italy, Germany, and even Great Britain—the collapse of prices is to-day more than all else embittering the relations between the governors and the governed, is held to justify the admission into legislation of methods of a perverted socialism, and is leading up rapidly to a complete reconstruction of political parties. Then we shall see emerge a Socialist Party on a Socialist "platform"—a Party which will claim to be the heir of all the Ages, and will revivify economic science on a basis of scientific socialism.

VII.

THE TWO GROUPS OF "BIMETALLISTS."

Much capital has been made out of the want of unanimity on the part of the currency reformers, and the intelligent spectator begins to fear that the patient will die of anœmia while two schools of doctors are wrangling at his bedside. Every objector to that legislation which during the quarter of a century after 1820 until the occurrence of the phenomenal gold discoveries in 1849 had all but ruined the agricultural interest in Great Britain, although that interest was protected up to the hilt by a tariff on imported foods; which was bringing about a collapse of the shipping and manufacturing industries, and which then as to-day had brought Ireland to the very brink of Civil War—every objector to this legislation is called a "bimetallist" by those who are too ignorant to recognize that it is only the term and not the theory which is unintelligent and unscientific. The science of money owes so much to the activity and researches of M. Henri Cernuschi that it would be ungracious to say more than that, while his science is faultless, his invention of a term so wanting in precision was unfortunate. However, the name "bimetallist" has gone out to the world, and a growing child owes much to its parent which is not included in the christening ceremony. The "bimetallists" then consider that unity of standard is important to the stability of trade. The monometallists, on the other hand, support the present system, a system of *two distinct standards of value within one Empire.* We have a silver standard in India, a gold standard in England. It would be by comparison much more convenient to have a silver standard in Yorkshire, and a gold standard in Lancashire. The inconvenience of the two standards system clearly varies *directly*, and not, as some apologists of the present system seem to hold, *inversely*, as the distance: for between England and India, the uncertainty of exchange to the Manchester merchant is not the uncertainty that exists to-day: the cable informs him to-day that the fifteen rupees for which he can sell a piece of cloth will exchange for a sovereign; but thirty days later, when his goods are delivered and the rupees paid, what portion of a sovereign are those rupees worh then? Well, that will depend, not at all on any fluctuations in the supply of silver from the world's mines, but upon contingencies impossible to foresee—a rumour that certain monetary legislation is contemplated at Washington, or that during the interval Mr. Goschen has said something complimentary about silver, or because Sir Evelyn Baring rather than Mr. Fowler is believed to have made the better impression on the minds of the Currency Commissioners. Upon accidents such as these the profit of British Trade is dependent to-day! But we are told there need be no such uncertainty as to the gold value of these fifteen rupees, that if the merchant wishes to eliminate the speculative element, instead of taking his chances of the state of exchange thirty days later when his goods arrive—then his banker will do the gambling in his place. He has only to give his banker threepence, and the banker will give him a sovereign and take the chance of any loss that may result from a further fall in exchange. It is true, indeed, that if the opponents of the Bland Bill are making a fresh disturbance at Washington, and the newspapers which represent the great Money Power are professing a firm conviction that the Bland Act will be forthwith repealed, then, indeed, exchange will fall in advance of business done, and the banker will require not threepence but perhaps a shilling in the pound. Like the rate of insurance, the premium is in proportion to the risk, but the man who proceeded to put up powder works in a wooden shed with defective fire flues would find his profits sadly diminished by the protection he buys from his insurance office. If legislation were to deny him the right to construct a fire-proof building, it would do precisely what legislation has done for the cotton industries of Lancashire. In the case of Silver-using countries, such as India and China, trading with one another, there is to-day no such charge for insurance, and the amount of this insurance is therefore an addition not merely to profits, but to *net profits*.

But what are the lines which divide the two Bimetallic camps? The differences are, I believe, not differences of principle, but merely differences of policy; and also the differences are just those which might be anticipated from the fact that two parties are demanding Currency Reform, and are watching their objective, from two distinct standpoints. There are on the one hand the assertors of Mill's "Quantity Theory" of Money, business men who have neither the time nor the inclination to study the "Silver Question" with that minuteness which is evident in the writings of Cernuschi or Arendt, Hermann Schmidt, Dana Horton and others; nor, I believe, to popularize the currency question is it at present desirable to do more than merely demonstrate that the rapid diminution of the stock of Gold in currency in England would of itself account for the present fall of prices: that whereas ten years since we had 140 millions of sovereigns, to-day we have scarcely more than one hundred millions. If we have thus lost thirty per cent. in ten years, how long will it take at this rate to drain us of all our Gold? If prices have fallen thirty per cent. already, why are we not now on the brink of a further and a more disastrous fall still? This is not the Silver Question but the Gold Question, and this is the view of prices which is taken by the majority of those who are anxious for currency reform. That majority has neither the time nor the desire to enter upon the metaphysics of the question; it is enough if we recognize that if the State undertakes the duty of deciding what is and what is not legal tender Money, and if Gold has become clearly insufficient in volume to support a steady range of prices, that then it is the business of the legislatures to act, and not to sit still on the chance that a new El Dorado may be discovered, as was the case in 1849.

Some authorities consider that issues of legal tender paper in the form of one pound notes not represented by Gold or Silver in reserve, would avail to remedy the contraction of the legal tender currency. But such a makeshift as this I believe would be wholly mischievous. Pound notes *representing Gold in reserve*, while exercising no influence whatever on prices, would form a convenient kind of currency, and would save the sovereigns they represent from loss of weight by friction, that is all: but beyond this an issue of ten millions of pound notes, *not* represented by Gold in reserve, would serve merely to slightly expand the currency at home, and would therefore raise prices in *Great Britain alone*. And the effect of such a rise of prices in a Free Trade country is to immediately increase the volume of the imports of that country, without any corresponding increase in exports. These augmented imports would require to be paid for, not in pound notes but in Gold; the effect therefore of the issue of ten millions of unsecured paper money would be to drive out of England an equivalent number of sovereigns, so that instead of stopping our present drain of Gold, the proposed issue of pound notes would accelerate that result.

We now come to the Silver Question, and to the position taken by the other school of reformers.

M. Henri Cernuschi and his disciples consider that the present distress and the fall of prices *may be* entirely independent of the alleged scarcity of Gold; and M. Cernuschi would declare with truth that even were another California to be discovered, so that the tendency was toward cheaper Gold and a rise of prices in Gold countries, yet that any such anti-silver legislation as that of Germany in 1873, originating this time at Washington or Paris, might more than neutralize the effect of the fresh Gold discoveries, and might even force down prices to a still lower level; that is to say, the tendency of the ratio between the metals would be to close up in consequence of the cheapening of Gold, formerly scarcer, but now more abundant; but on the other hand the new *legislative restrictions* on the employment of Silver in the currencies might even further widen the ratio, and bring about a further dislocation in international trade.

Let me state the position in this way: we have

in England a hundred million sovereigns to-day; suppose the new mines in Wales which we read of gave us a further hundred millions within the next six months, the tendency would clearly be for all prices in England to be doubled; wheat now selling for three half sovereigns a quarter might sell for three sovereigns. But on the other hand, suppose not only that the Bland Act was suspended, but that the United States and France throw their Silver upon the market to be sold for what it would fetch. Clearly the rupee would tend to fall towards six pence. And if the rupee were to fall, what must be the effect on the price of English wheat? The ryot, if the value of Silver in India to buy commodities remained the same, would require only 23 rupees a quarter to return him a fair profit; therefore, as I mentioned in an earlier chapter, the great fall in the price of Silver would so stimulate wheat exports from India that, notwithstanding the tendency of the Welsh Gold to effect a rapid rise of prices in England, the still more rapid fall in the price of the rupee would force down English wheat prices to a point even lower than before. It is not the scarcity of Gold which M. Cernuschi dreads, nor perhaps has he ever put himself on record as opposed to a fall of prices, so long as that fall is *an universal fall*. But in his view, what is making Trade, and especially Free Trade, impossible, is Western monetary legislation which has sufficed to force down Gold prices locally, to the confusion of industry in the West, but which as yet has been powerless to alter the level of Silver prices in the great Silver-using Nations of the East. And this is why M. Cernuschi and others attach such importance to a fixed ratio between Silver and Gold, without which what is termed the par of exchange between Europe and the great Nations of the East cannot be maintained.

And this brings us to a consideration of the most disputed question in the entire domain of Economic Science—the question of the Fixed Ratio; whether it is possible to maintain a Fixed Ratio, whether, if possible, it is just and necessary to fix such a ratio by international agreement.

VIII.

THE FIXED RATIO—IS IT PRACTICABLE?

THERE are great numbers of intelligent people who recognize both the distress which has followed from the recent fall of prices, and that this fall is mainly attributable to certain novel conditions in the world's currencies introduced by the process of recent legislation. But though the disease is very evident, there are grave doubts as to the nature of the remedy. It is clear that if instead of a single legal tender, we are to have two legal tenders current side by side, the two metals must bear a certain ratio to one another. Now what is this ratio to be? The origin of the word money (pecunia) was in the legal tender of cattle (pecus), and if the State to-day were to determine that all debts might be paid at the option of the debtor in bullocks or in sheep at the ratio of one bullock to two sheep, the State would clearly have established a ratio of 1 to 2 between the values of bullocks and sheep. But could the State maintain this ratio? Clearly the

THE FIXED RATIO—IS IT PRACTICABLE? 91

State could not; the cost of producing a bullock is much more than the cost of producing two sheep, because a larger expenditure of labour, time, and food has been incurred in the case of the bullock. Therefore if the State declared such a ratio of value as 1 to 2 between bullocks and sheep, the loss on producing cattle would be on such a scale that every one would either breed sheep or at least find some other employment than cattle raising. The reason, and the only reason, why the State could not establish a ratio between cattle and sheep, or between potatoes and pineapples, is this—their cost of production varies from time to time, and therefore the price of potatoes as compared with the price of pineapples must vary as their cost of production varies. And for similar reasons all the earlier economists—Ricardo, Mill, and others—and even so recent a writer as Jevons, have assumed that the price also of the precious metals was controlled by their cost of production. For this reason, and for no other, they decided that bimetallism was unscientific; that whichever of the metals came to be undervalued would no longer be produced; and that therefore no fixed ratio could be maintained. But as to this all-important point, what has been the evidence accumulated during the past ten years? The experts, while they differ as to the exact figures of cost, are all agreed that the cost of producing either an ounce of silver or an ounce of gold is much more than the value of those ounces when they have been produced. Herein, then, is the great difference between the production of the precious metals and the production of turnips. The total world's outlay in producing gold and silver is greater than the money value of the two metals produced. The total outlay on turnips is less, taking one year with another, than the money value of the turnip crop. It is some two thousand years since a poet wrote of the *auri sacra fames.* He had clearly in his mind a tendency in human nature which was at variance with the laws of economic science. It would never have occurred to him to write of the "divine hunger" for turnips! At that time the precious metals in the Roman Empire were being produced entirely by slave-labour under the stimulus of the lash. When there were no longer fresh nations for Rome to conquer and enslave, the production of the precious metals for hundreds of years ceased entirely. Jacob states that in the reign of Augustus, about the time of the nativity of Christ, there were current in the Roman Empire 328 millions sterling of metallic money—three times the stock England holds to-day, while at the commencement of the 9th century this mass had been reduced to 33 millions only—*to less than one-tenth!* Not without reason does Allison declare that the collapse of the Roman Empire is to be attributed to this prodigious contraction of currency and prices.

It may seem at first sight incredible that humanity should in these philosophic days continue to produce gold and silver at a loss; but the life of the gold-seeker is a life often of intense excitement; the attraction is that of the gambling table intensified; the blanks are indeed many, but the prizes though few are very valuable. The hundred lose all they possess, and perhaps an entire life's work, but the one becomes a millionnaire. In the spring of 1879 I visited the town of Leadville in Colorado. The previous year some rich deposits of silver carbonates had been discovered, and a few working miners had realized suddenly large fortunes. The result was a rush to Leadville from all parts of the world, so that a large town had in a few months sprung up as from the wand of the magician on the very summit of the Rocky Mountains, more than a hundred miles from any railway. Fifty thousand people were at that time encamped there almost within the line of perpetual snow. Now here was the recent instance of a large town built solely for the purposes of the silver mines, while enormous numbers of men, withdrawn from other productive industries, were being employed at very high wages in the mines. Hay was selling for £50 per ton : all other things proportionately high. During the "boom times" at Leadville, it is possible that the output of silver may have been equal in value to the wages, say £20,000 a day, paid in the town ; but taking into consideration the enormous sums of money sunk ni the mine-shafts and in the building of this now half deserted town, it is certain that the silver produced even at Leadville was produced at a great loss. Nor was this all. The excitement of the discoveries at Leadville made itself felt in every State and every territory within the district of the Rocky Mountains: thousands of working men abandoned their ordinary pursuits, and swarmed into the nearest hills, having sold their homesteads and invested all their savings in the purchase of pack-horses and mining tools.

Such is the result of every fresh discovery of the precious metals. It was said that at one time the great Nevada "bonanza," the Comstock silver mine, was producing silver at the rate of eighteen pence per ounce, silver being at that time worth sixty pence: the excitement was in consequence intense, and reflected itself in a widening circle all over the world. But so far from bringing down the cost of producing silver, I have no doubt that the real effect was quite the contrary. By increasing the number of those who were seeking the precious minerals, it doubtless immediately *raised* very largely the universal average cost of producing the ounce of silver. The United States produce annually about ten millions sterling of silver. If it were possible to procure exact returns of the number of men not merely working in the mines, but of the far larger number who are hunting for fresh mines, who are building mining camps and roads and bridges to mining towns in the most inaccessible regions—the expenditure also on horses and mules and other locomotive power—on the tools, the machinery, the smelters, and the fuel for those smelters, it would be found that Mr. del Mar's estimate that it costs three dollars to procure a dollar's worth of silver is well within the mark.

Now if it is once admitted that the cost of

producing the precious metals is more than their value when produced, it is clear that any difficulty as to fixing the ratio between their values at once disappears. If the cost of producing is to-day so far against the miner that *merely economic reasons* should already have driven him into other occupations, then to declare a fixed ratio between gold and silver need not, within certain limits, discourage the silver miner and encourage the gold miner. The more so when we consider that most silver mines also produce gold, and *vice versâ*. The greatest silver mine the world has ever known is the Comstock, and yet nearly forty per cent. of its entire yield of bullion was gold.

Of course, if legislation went the length of declaring a ratio of 1 to 1 or even 1 to 4, the man who is to-day gold-seeking would give it up, finding it somewhat less unprofitable to abandon gold and turn his attention to silver. The immense over-valuation of silver at a ratio of 1 to 1 would be apparent. But any ratio between the limits of 1 to 7 and 1 to 30 would probably not withdraw labour from the production of one metal rather than the other; and it may, therefore, be entirely practicable for the State to fix any ratio between these wide limits. As a matter of policy perhaps the ratio should favour silver rather than gold, because while gold-seeking in the river-beds requires little or no outlay, silver-mining on the other hand, which involves shafting and quartz-crushing, offers less attraction to the ordinary miner, who is not a capitalist, and therefore silver-mining requires a more direct encouragement from the State. For this reason, if the world were beginning all over again, the ratio of 1 to 10 would seem to be preferable to the immortal 1 to $15\frac{1}{2}$, so beloved of M. Cernuschi and his school. Assuming however that the money metals are produced at a dead loss, there is clearly nothing impracticable in a fixed ratio.

It may be said that if the bringing of the precious metals to the surface involves such a huge waste of human labour, it is the duty of the State to discourage production by demonetizing one or even both of the metals. But on the other hand metallic money is of all the machinery of civilization the most necessary. As Wolowski has well said, "Of all human agencies money is that one which costs the least for the work it performs;" and I think when all things are considered, the two metals, silver and gold, comply with the requirements of a standard of value not in spite of, but even *in consequence of*, the fact that because their production entails an annual loss, their price is not determined by their "cost of production," and they can therefore *jointly* perform the function of legal tender.

It remains, however, further to consider the question as to what the ratio should be, and here we have arrived at the very thickest of the fight around the standards. What is the present duty of the State to its citizens where interests—pocket interests—are found to be diametrically opposed?

IX.

THE FIXED RATIO—ITS PROPORTION.

IF we trace the comparative values of gold and silver for the past seven hundred years, we shall find that the ratio has varied suddenly and considerably twice only—once at the close of the thirteenth century, and again in the past twelve years. On each occasion the variation cannot be attributed to natural laws, but to the effect of monetary legislation. Professor Thorold Rogers has established that in 1262 the ratio of gold to silver in Europe was as 1 to $9\frac{5}{8}$, whereas in 1292 gold had so appreciated in relation to silver that the ratio was as 1 to $12\frac{1}{2}$. It appears that Venice, which at that time was the leading trading community in Europe, had about 1270 commenced to discard silver and to buy and coin gold ducats instead, and that the example of Venice had been followed, at least as far as a gold currency was concerned, by the coining of gold pieces in Hungary and at Brescia and Florence.

As to the violent changes of ratio in the last twelve years, which no one now questions have been the result of the anti-silver legislation of Germany in 1873, the consequent stoppage of the coinage of silver in France and the immense drain of gold to the United States in consequence of the monetary legislation in that country—as to these changes, I have considered them fully in the earlier chapters of this volume. Enough to say that mere *alterations in the supply of the precious metals*, when the mints of the Western nations have been freely open to both metals, have not been sufficient at any time to cause any variation in the ratio. In 1846 the output of gold was six millions, that of silver six millions and a half. Six years later the output of gold had increased to 30 millions; the output of silver had risen to 8½ millions. Although a similar disparity of production continued for many years, there was yet no disturbance of the ratio itself, which, owing to the bimetallic action of France, was steady all the world over at 1 to 15½. Then occurred the legislation complained of, with the result that in fifteen years the ratio of 1 to 15½ has widened, until it is to-day as 1 to 21.

But now the question is how can we undo the harm done by hasty or dishonest legislation without dealing unfairly with contracts recently entered into between debtor and creditor? It is easy to agree that in view of the recent disturbance of trades, if the ratio were once again restored to $15\frac{1}{2}$, then the Western nations would be wise to open their mints to the free coinage of both metals at that ratio. But there is at present a hideous gap between the old ratio and the present values of bullion. How can it be closed up? At this point M. Cernuschi assures us that if an international monetary conference agreed to admit silver to free coinage at 1 to $15\frac{1}{2}$, no creditor would lose; that he would be as well off as though paid in gold or in the silver equivalent to that gold. Silver, M. Cernuschi considers, would immediately rise in value, its lawful historic prerogative of legal tender money being again restored to it. I have not done justice to M. Cernuschi in stating his position thus shortly; and further, I recognize my inability to do him entire justice on this point. But what is of the first importance, the reasoning faculty of the man in the street is not equal to this bimetallic subtlety, and before bimetallism can win the day, we have to carry with us the man in the street. For one man who at present follows M. Cernuschi, ten men are repelled by this proposal to refix the old ratio in defiance of the present market price of silver. The ten say, "We are owed £20—say five ounces of gold—that gold is to-day worth 105 ounces of silver, whereas you wish to pay us off with only 77½ ounces! Are we then Irish landlords that we are to be treated after such fashion?" To recommend to these ten creditors a study of Cernuschi's writings is useless. At least nine-tenths of them, however, stand ready to receive their five ounces of gold, *or the silver equivalent to that gold* (that is, 105 ounces), if the State has previously declared silver to be legal tender money for all taxes and debts; only the incorrigible Gold Bug, the man who desires to contract the currency by legislation, so that he may get rich at his neighbour's expense, will object to this action of the State at a time when it is so clearly necessary in order to protect the general community against a vast further fall of prices.

We may assume, therefore, that if the Parliament of England said to-morrow, "You can all pay your debts in gold, or in the silver equivalent to that gold at the market price of silver for the time obtaining, and we will, as a matter of convenience, issue notes representing all the silver that is brought to the mints," no one would have the right to object to legislation which takes not one penny out of the pockets of any one, and which is clearly required by the present contracted condition of the currency—a contraction rapidly intensifying. Such legislation would no doubt be furiously opposed by one class, but would meet with the approval of nine-tenths of the community. There is no difficulty at any time in ascertaining the price of silver. The Indian Council sells to the highest bidder more than a quarter of a million sterling in council drafts every week. The price of these drafts, of course, sets the price of silver bullion. Now, suppose that silver was declared legal tender in Great Britain for unlimited sums at the ratio of 1 to 21, then clearly the price of silver could never fall lower. There are more than four thousand millions sterling of debts in Great Britain, and only a little more than a hundred millions sterling of metallic legal tender, so that any tendency of silver to depreciate would, at any time, be neutralized by the desire of men to pay their debts in the cheaper metal. England therefore having "put in the peg" below which silver could not fall, this would at once happen: in France to-day is more than a hundred millions sterling of legal tender silver which was coined at the ratio of 1 to $15\frac{1}{2}$. That is to say, the silver of which a five-franc piece is composed can be bought for less than four francs. This being the case, an inducement in the shape of a premium of 25 per cent. exists for individuals to fraudulently coin legal tender silver. In the *uttering* of these coins there is no risk whatever, their intrinsic value being equal to that of any five-franc piece issued by the mint. Quite recently an issue of Sicilian dollars was called in, when it was found that more of these dollars were returned to the State than had ever been issued by the State. It is generally believed also that many "Bland" dollars have been coined in the United States in this way on " private account."

Such a state of things as this must be very inconvenient to Italy, France, the United States, and Germany, and it is certain that the action of England in making silver legal tender at 1 to 21 would be promptly followed by action on the part of these countries to restore their old ratio. And the restoration could be quickly effected in this way: the price of silver next week will depend on the price at which some quarter of a million sterling of advertised council drafts will be sold in London. The French Government, in order to restore the bullion value of their own immense stock of silver to par with gold, would

THE FIXED RATIO—ITS PROPORTION.   105

no doubt send an agent to London to bid up the price of council drafts to the old silver value of $60\frac{3}{4}$ pence per ounce: a few thousands of pounds would suffice for this purpose, once the price was put up, silver being still legal tender in England at its market ratio to gold, silver could never again fall below 1 to $15\frac{1}{2}$, for the same reason that it could never fall below 1 to 21—on account of the demand of the great debtor class, which would wish to pay its debts in whichever metal tended to become cheaper. And if the Bank of France did not seize this opportunity, this would be immediately done by private enterprise. The exporting merchants of London and Liverpool would buy "forward exchange" from their bankers to the amount of some millions sterling, and would then bid up the exchange till the old value of the rupee was restored. The profits on this transaction would be immense: loss would be impossible. And the ratio once restored to 1 to $15\frac{1}{2}$, it is clear that it could never rise higher, say to 1 to 12, because just as France did after the great gold discoveries, so she would again do—she would buy and coin that metal which tended to become cheaper; and if the ratio of gold to silver came to less than 1 to $15\frac{1}{2}$, she would sell her silver and replace it with gold, thereby establishing the ratio as long as there was any legal tender gold at all left in Germany, in England, or the United States.

Such is the automatic action of bimetallism; silver cannot become cheaper, because if there was any such tendencies the demand of the debtor classes would suffice to restore it. For the same reason neither can gold become cheaper; therefore absolute stability of the ratio is maintained. And as things are, that ratio can be none other than the ratio of 1 to 15½, not because there is anything *natural* in such a ratio, but because it has been so fixed by generations of past legislators and by the accumulation of masses of legal tender silver coined at that ratio during hundreds of years. It is this mass of legal tender silver which can always be relied upon to absorb any smaller mass coined at any other ratio, if, and only if, silver is permitted its former prerogative of free coinage and legal tender.

I am aware that this proposal—the making of silver legal tender at its gold value—a proposal made by Mr. Warner in the United States and by Earl Grey in England—is opposed to the orthodox bimetallic platform. But on the other hand it has always appeared to me that solution which will attract to the monetary reform movement the most ready support from the general community. It has been suggested, but without sufficient reason, that the ratio would, under this operation, crystallize at 1 to 21; but the lesson of the past has been quite otherwise. When the ratio in the United States was 1 to 15, silver was found to be overvalued, and was melted and sent abroad to be sold for gold. The ratio was accordingly altered to 1 to 16, at which ratio gold was overvalued and left the country. Nor could it be otherwise if we opened our mints to free coinage at 1 to 21. The price of silver would rise, other Western nations would commence to coin, and the historic ratio of 1 to $15\frac{1}{2}$ would be restored probably in a very few days.

If this view is correct, then there is no need for England to wait for the action of any international monetary convention. She can alone and unaided restore the "par of exchange" and terminate the existing depression of Trade and Prices.

X.

INDIA AND THE SILVER QUESTION.

In considering Mr. David Wells's views on bi-metallism I drew attention to the fact that each fresh fall in the price of silver stimulates the exports of Indian wheat and other produce to Great Britain. In other words, the Indian exporter can sell his wheat profitably in Mark Lane for 22 rupees; these 22 rupees for which he formerly paid two sovereigns, he can now buy for three half-sovereigns. Clearly it may be such a condition of exchange as this which is to-day destroying the profits of English agriculture.

And while the maxim of the Manchester cotton spinner, who can neither afford to stop his machinery nor disperse his hands, is "business at any price," it is evident that he, too, must suffer not less than the farmer by a fall in the exchange value of the rupee. His Indian customer, the up-country merchant of Delhi or Agra, desires to buy cotton goods for rupees, and if the rupee is worth 20d. in Manchester, this customer can buy a certain piece of cotton cloth for 100 rupees, but if the rupee falls to its present price 17d., then the same piece of cloth will cost 114 rupees. Now, while the Bombay mills may be unable to manufacture this piece of cloth for 100 rupees, yet its cost of production may be slightly less than 114 rupees; therefore, whether this merchant's order goes to Manchester or to Bombay will be decided by the fluctuating value of the rupee. And the fact that Bombay is now doing an immense proportion of the trade in yarns to China which was formerly done by Manchester, may be fairly referred to the recent currency disturbance. Of course there is the other view of it—that it is economical to manufacture yarns where labour is cheap, and the cotton itself is produced, rather than to send the raw material four thousand miles to Manchester from Bombay, and after manufacturing bring the yarns back again. But Mr. J. G. Scott has met this argument very fairly. He points out that while the Manchester spinner buys his coal at 8s., the cost of coal in Bombay averages 24s. per ton, that each ton of yarn requires for its manufacture more than two tons of coal; owing, therefore, to the cheapness of coal, the English manufacturer of yarns is at an advantage of 32s. per each ton of yarn as compared with the Bombay manufacturer. The steamship charges on a ton of cotton from Bombay to Manchester are 22*s.*, upon the ton of yarn from Manchester to Bombay 12*s.* 6*d.*, so that looking at the China trade the economy in freight charges in favour of Bombay is fairly offset by the economy in coal in favour of Manchester. Again, owing to the higher price of coal, boilers in Bombay are worked at much higher pressure, and, therefore, only last half as long as in England. The salary of a manager in a Bombay mill is from £80 to £100 per month as compared with £16 in Manchester. The Government of India further requires that only certificated engineers at salaries which average £40 a month should be employed in the Indian mills, while the engineer in a Manchester mill receives only £6 a month. For these and other reasons Mr. Scott believes that the cheaper labour of Bombay, and the propinquity to China, are not of themselves sufficient to account for the phenomenal growth of the yarn trade between India and China.

But such a condition of exchange as the present, when silver seems destined to fall steadily and continuously, is considered by many high authorities to be beneficial to India, even though this benefit is secured at the expense of England, and, however erroneous this view, I must admit that it was a view I used fully to share. And there are many who to-day consider that because a continuous decline in the value of silver stimulates Indian exports, it would therefore be unfair to sacrifice the East to the West, by a monetary convention which in admitting silver to legal tender would increase the coinage demand for silver and raise its price. It is clear, however, in the first place that only a very small portion of the trade of India—her export trade—can benefit by the stimulus afforded by the fall in the exchange, and however many fallacies may be discerned amongst the axioms of the free traders, this at least holds good, that in considering international trade between two countries such as England and India, which exchange freely with each other, any condition of exchange which may be detrimental to the one cannot be beneficial to the other. The original idea of free trade was this and this only—that as some men possess a special aptitude for making hats, while others make boots more cheaply, it is therefore for the well-being of the world that the makers of cheap hats should exchange freely with the makers of cheap boots, and this theory of exchange applies as well to nations as to individuals. But if the right arm of the man who makes hats is to be tied up, then he can neither make hats so cheaply, nor give so many hats as before in exchange for boots. In consequence of the dislocation in the par of exchange, England, with her right hand disabled, is still protesting that she trades freely with India. Thus it has come about that English manufacturers are finding the margin of their profit vanishing, and while the Asiatic myriads have become unprofitable customers, our home trade is also languishing from a perpetual contraction of prices, and also from the destruction of the landed interest. The depression flowing from this source has spread from one business to another, till it has affected every industry in the country. Therefore, while the cheap rupee may be directly benefiting certain export trades, yet indirectly it is contracting India's market area abroad, by diminishing the general prosperity of nations which are customers for Indian produce. And, in another direction, India clearly suffers; she has borrowed immense sums of money in England to build railroads and other public works: the interest on this money is fixed in terms of gold; where formerly 10 rupees would pay a sovereign in interest, now 14 rupees are required; each fall of a penny in the exchange value of the rupee involves a loss of a million sterling to the Indian revenue. The present value of the rupee accounts therefore for a loss of more than five millions of revenue; and while the revenue has thus diminished, or, to be more correct, while taxation has been thus increased, it is not equally clear that the profits of the Indian export trades have absorbed even the amount of the increased taxation. It is on the contrary quite possible that two rupees are being taken from the pocket of the community in the form of increased taxes, in order to give one to a class—a very small class—the exporting merchants. The annual gross exports of India are some fifty millions sterling; it is hardly probable that the profits on this trade are as high as 20 per cent., or ten millions, and to secure this sum of ten millions of profit against a possible reduction—to secure for it that bonus now afforded by the depreciated rupee, the community is asked to pay five millions sterling in increased taxation; the salt-tax has to be increased, and while every Anglo-Indian official finds his salary diminished by the imposition of an Indian income-tax, a further income-tax of nearly five shillings in the pound awaits him on every sovereign of his savings which he requires to remit to England.

Let us admit freely what the monometallists now claim, that the present relations between the two metals do stimulate the exports of Indian wheat to England and of Indian yarns to China, and that the more the ratio widens the greater will be the stimulus to Indian exports. Let us even suppose that one-half of the entire export trade of India is clear profit, and results from the depreciation of silver, then there is a sum of 25 millions sterling which goes into the pockets of certain Indian merchants, less only five millions the amount of the increased taxes. Is it then to the advantage of India to continue the present currency condition for the sake of this twenty millions of supposed bonus? I believe not. I believe that the evident stimulus to the mere *export trades* of any country which is clearly the result of a depreciating currency whether of silver or paper, is offset ten times over by the losses and uncertainties which must occur in the channels of the *domestic trade* of that country. The annual production of wealth in India probably aggregates to at least a thousand millions sterling, which sum is only one-half of the wealth estimated to be produced annually in the United

States by a population numbering one-fourth only that of India, and which pays only about an equal revenue to the State. Is the present condition of the Indian currency sacrificing the interests of the producers of nine hundred and fifty millions consumed at home, for the benefit of the producers of fifty millions sent abroad? I must leave the consideration of this question for another chapter, merely mentioning in advance that the general opinion of the export merchants themselves seems to be that while they do not profit considerably by the decline in exchange, the impossibility of realizing their capital and remitting it home without immense loss, far outweighs the benefit of the bonus afforded to exports. As far as the outer world is concerned the fall of prices resulting from the depreciation of silver is bringing losses immensely greater than the advantages supposed to be secured by India. As is always the case when bonused imports are admitted freely, the rival producers who receive a million of bonus are able, by destroying the profits of our home trade for a few years, to displace an entire industry, to destroy also tens of millions of fixed capital locked up in that industry; and this I believe to be the case with the bonus afforded by the cheap rupee. Not only is the capital of the English farmer being swept away, but the land through being neglected has become unsaleable, and this deplorable condition of things dates back to the silver crisis which commenced in 1875. The amount of the fall in the price of wheat which has been brought about by the fall in the price of silver, Mr. Inglis Palgrave, the late editor of the *Economist*, declares to be at the rate of 17*d*. per quarter for each penny the rupee has fallen—in all to some seven shillings a quarter. It must be remembered that the three to four million quarters of wheat which India exports to Europe, absolutely settles the price of wheat in the Mark Lane market. The Indian exporter can afford to sell his wheat for 22 rupees per quarter; the competition of other Indian producers must always avail to keep prices down to that point, and, therefore, the English and the American farmer must also sell his wheat in Mark Lane for the gold equivalent of 22 rupees, that is, for thirty shillings. If, then, we admit that the English market is the objective of all wheat-growers—that it is on this market that the American, the Indian, and the Russian relies to dispose of any surplus crop—then it is clear that the price of the world's wheat is decided by the price of wheat in Mark Lane, and the price of wheat in Mark Lane is set by the fact that the Indian ryot can afford to sell a quarter of wheat there for eight ounces of silver. In other words, the price of wheat is controlled by the price of silver.

A very able article on wheat-growing appeared in the *Quarterly Review* for April, 1887. The writer drew attention to the fact that while wheat in England has for years past been produced at an admitted loss, the position of the wheat-grower in the United States is no better than in England. And, although this statement has been contested with much ability by Mr. Edward Atkinson, the weight of the evidence seems to be on the side of the *Quarterly Review*. From my own observations in the Western States of America, I am convinced that the wheat farmers of Kansas, Nebraska, Minnesota, and Dakota have suffered enormous losses, and that these States have only avoided an agricultural collapse more complete even than that in England because of the large local disbursements of money to build new railroads in those States. It is worthy of notice that during the past twelve months no less than *four thousand miles* of railway have been constructed within the three States of Kansas, Nebraska, and Dakota, at a cost approximating twenty millions sterling. Of this sum probably one-half may have been spent on land labour and local produce within those States, thus raising prices locally and increasing profits. But when a " boom " of this temporary nature has passed by it will be impossible for the Americans to continue to export wheat at anything approaching present prices; they have already, owing to the fall of prices, largely contracted their area under wheat, and are turning their attention to the production of meat and dairy produce, with the result that the prices of these exports also have been forced down by American competition, to the confusion of Irish "judicial" rents, and to the destruction of a social system.

Thus the fall not in wheat prices only, but also in the price of meat, and other agricultural produce, is to be traced directly to the present position of silver.

XI.

INDIA AND THE SILVER QUESTION (*continued*).

THE prodigies of production which the 19th century has revealed to us may be referred to two concurrent causes: (1) The developments of modern machinery, and (2) the cheapness of loanable capital under the conditions of modern credit. It would be difficult to decide which of these two has been the more important factor in the mighty results we have been permitted to witness.

How is it that the manufacturers of Europe and of America can be induced to continue to manufacture when prices are so low, and the margin of profit so extremely small? How is it that when the net profits of trade have been reduced to a margin of eight per cent., yet the profits of the manufacturers are twenty per cent.— are actually greater than when the profit margin was nominally twelve per cent. instead of eight? This problem does not involve any startling paradox. Suppose a man with ten thousand pounds of his own connects himself with such an industry as, for instance, the shipping or cotton spinning trade. He requires £50,000 for his plant and operating expenses; the balance of forty thousand he is able to borrow upon the security of his own capital and the plant at say four and a half per cent.: now if the net profit of his business is eight per cent., he earns £4,000 a year, less 4 per cent. on £40,000, or £1,800: so that his net profit on his original £10,000 amounts to £2,200, or 22 per cent. per annum. Owing to the fact that he is able to borrow money at $4\frac{1}{2}$ per cent. rather than eight, he is able also to secure such a rate of profit as keeps him actively engaged and satisfied to remain in business, and he is able to pay the wages of brisk business times to the labourers he employs. Now it is clear that if the loan rate of money was 8 per cent., then, unless he sold his goods at a much higher price and so obtained a much higher margin of profit than 8 per cent. on each sale, this manufacturer would retire from active business and would prefer to be a lender of money rather than a borrower.

Now herein is, as it appears to me, the entire crux of this Silver Question with reference to

India. Solely and entirely in consequence of the exchange difficulty—of the fact that a western capitalist who converts gold into silver, for the purpose of making loans in India, never knows when or to what extent in consequence of a further fall in exchange, his sovereigns may come back to him in diminished numbers—solely in consequence of this insecurity, the market price of money loaned on first class mortgage security, for one year, two or five years is at least as high as 7 per cent. per annum throughout British India. It has indeed come to this point, that British Trustees are no longer permitted to invest trust moneys in India at all! Can any one suggest any other than the currency reason for the present rate which can be obtained for money in India? If money is to-day being loaned freely at 3 per cent. on land mortgages in London, why is it that such a rate as 7 per cent. can be obtained on mortgage of the most valuable and constantly improving building sites in the City of Bombay? The only possible explanation is, I think, the natural feeling of insecurity occasioned by a falling rate of exchange. If money in India was 50 per cent. cheaper to borrow—was as cheap for example as it is in Manchester, then without the advantage resulting from a depreciated currency, it seems to me that the cotton mills of Bombay could still compete with the cotton mills of Manchester in supplying the China market; and in addition the one burning need of India and of England would be supplied —the East would be supplied with cheap capital, while at the same time the Western capitalist who is now forced to lend his money for $2\frac{1}{2}$ per cent. would obtain 4 per cent.; the Indian Government or the Indian producers who today borrow at 6 and 8 per cent. respectively would at once be able to borrow at 4; both parties, the borrower and lender also, would thus be suited, and while India would be developed, the benefit of her political connection with the richest country in the world would be made evident to the native mind.

At present, in consequence of the economic crisis—the Silver crisis—India might almost as well, as far as the blessing of cheap loanable money is concerned, be connected not with England but with the Turkish Empire. And how greatly it would emphasize the comparative advantage of English over Russian rule if we could show the native masses that the consequence of British rule is money at 4 per cent.—that, on the other hand, the cost of the Russian connection would be depreciating rouble paper and a 9 per cent. bank rate.

The point therefore to which this so-called "monometallic system"—a system of two disconnected standards of value within the bounds of one Empire—the point to which this system has brought this Empire may be summed up in these words.

In England an unhealthy glut of capital seeking investment and finding no remunerative demand;

But in India a money famine, high rates of interest, and a tardy development of her national resources.

In England our manufacturers and our farmers distracted by Indian exports bonused by the depreciating rupee;

But in India business conditions which are generally unprofitable because of money scarce and dear, excepting only in the case of a few highly-favoured, and so to speak "protected" export trades, which are a mere fraction of the entire trades of the Indian Peninsula.

In England low prices and an absence of all profit;

But in India prices high by comparison with those which would obtain with cheaper loanable capital: an insecure scale of profit, fluctuating between wide extremes, and subject to exchange gambling: a retarded railway development, insufficient irrigation, and a famine at hand.

Such are some of the fruits of the Gold Bugs' Creed.

XII.

DEPRECIATED CURRENCIES AND THEIR EFFECT ON PRICES.

THE recent further depreciation of the Russian Paper Currency, that is, the increased premium on gold in Russia, has brought the question of depreciated paper currencies again before the public attention. Any statement of the Currency Crisis would be incomplete which omitted to consider the effect on prices in countries which have a sound metallic currency, of exports from countries where an inconvertible paper currency is depreciating more or less rapidly. The question itself is of extreme importance, but has hitherto been so far neglected that there is very little if any statistical data which can be reliably used in this connection. At a recent meeting, however, of the Central Chamber of Agriculture, Mr. W. J. Harris shrewdly argued that, while quite recognizing the bonus to wheat exports from India afforded by the depreciating rupee, it would still be impolitic to correct this by any monetary agreement which would restore its value to silver, because the effect would be to shut off India's wheat exports to England and to permit their place to be taken by exports of wheat from Russia, where Mr. Harris declared from his own experience as a wheat importer, that although the rouble—just as the rupee in India—was depreciating, yet that this depreciation was not diminishing in Russia itself the purchasing power of rouble paper notes. As to his facts, Mr. Harris is borne out by much independent testimony. Colonel Le Mesurier assured me recently in Calcutta that in the trans-Caspian provinces of Russia this year he was obliged to exchange gold for rouble notes, paying a positive premium for the "depreciating" notes. As to Mr. Harris's conclusion, however, and his rejection of the bimetallic remedy, Mr. Harris is perhaps not wholly correct; for what is the increasing depreciation of the rouble, except another form of the statement that the premium on gold in Russia is increasing. Now such a depreciation of the currency of a country comes from one of two causes, or from both these causes operating together—(1) a paper inflation within the country itself, as was the case with assignats in France, or (2) a cause which is not local but universal—the growing comparative scarcity of international legal tender money. In the case of India at least, while the rupee has fallen some 25 per cent., this fall is clearly not owing to any currency inflation. India is on a metallic basis, and the fall in the rupee is nct, as I have before pointed out, owing to a fall in the value of silver, but to a rise in the value of gold. The remedy for this is evidently to increase the mass of international legal tender money, by making silver "good money"—the money of exchange. This rise in the value of silver would reduce the premium everywhere on gold; and similarly a rise in the value of silver, which is the standard within Russia, would also reduce the premium on gold in Russia—that is to say, would tend to correct the increasing depreciation of the rouble notes. I suppose therefore that of the amount of the present premium on gold in Russia (some 45 per cent.), at least 25 per cent. would disappear were its old value to be returned to silver. There would then, instead of a bonus of some 45 per cent. on Russian exports of wheat to England, be a bonus of not more than 20 per cent., a very serious condition of things if permanent, a condition which clearly entitles Mr.

Harris and others to raise the question whether Free Trade was ever intended to cover such a condition of exchange as this.

The further fall in the value of the Russian currency, which has necessarily been followed by a fall in the price of all Russian securities, should prove an additional incentive to Germany to support international bimetallism. The Russian securities are held in immense amounts by the Berlin banks, and if the gold premium in Russia is diminished Russian government securities will certainly rise.

But now it will be objected that if the fall in the rouble, as in the rupee, stimulates Russian exports, may it not be a good policy both in Russia and in other countries to inflate their currencies with inconvertible paper money, in order to swell the volume of their exports. But there can be no doubt that while under such conditions the mere export trade of a country may expand, yet the destruction of the National Credit, the fall in the value of its securities both at home and abroad, and the inevitable demoralization of all trades, if not in the remote interior, yet at least near the ports and the money centres—these causes of disturbance far more than outweigh any temporary advantage which may be obtained by a few exporting merchants. As I endeavoured to show was the case in India, the depreciation of the rupee by stimulating exports is a possible benefit to some five per cent. of the National Industries, at the expense of 95 per cent. of those industries. That exports stimulated in this way, and coming from countries with a depreciated currency, are destructive of the stability of trade and prices in countries such as England where the standard of value is appreciating—this is now universally conceded. But while this is a strong argument for National protection—self-protection—it is perfectly certain also that the offending—the inflating nation itself suffers.

And not alone is Russia an offender in this respect. The currency condition in the Argentine Republic in a similar manner stimulates the export trade of that country in beef, mutton, and wool, and also the cereals. And unlike Russia and India, where the depreciation has until quite recently been characterized by some steadiness, the gold premium in the Argentine ranges from zero to 50 per cent. within a period of a few months. This is the result no doubt of large frequent borrowings of gold in London and Paris; but the merchants of

Liverpool have come to make a profitable forecast of these exchange fluctuations, and are able thereby to secure very large profits from time to time. For example Messrs. Nelsons, the leading meat salesmen of Liverpool, are able, as the premium on gold at Buenos Ayres rises, to buy for one hundred sovereigns £150 or more of the paper currency of the Argentine: this sum invested in sheep within that country will clearly buy as many sheep as £150 would buy when the paper currency is at par with gold, for just as is the case with the rupee in India, so also in the Argentine Republic, merchants are agreed that local prices are not disturbed *pari passu* with the fluctuations of the paper currency—that prices, in short, are controlled by the local paper money, and are almost independent of the increase or the diminution of the premium on gold.

XIII.

THE SOCIALISM OF TO-MORROW.

To carry the intention of this book to completion, it is necessary not only to point out the effects of class legislation in inducing the present Economic Crisis, but also to consider by what means the community may in future protect itself against the inequalities of distribution which have been induced by this legislation.

The rapid spread of Socialism on the continent of Europe and in America; the growing disregard of those established principles which have hitherto controlled the law-makers, and the breaking up everywhere and the re-grouping of political parties; the revolt also, whether against economic science itself, or against the admitted excesses of its professors—these and many other symptoms of a vague unrest in the public mind are accumulating evidence that large social changes are at hand, and that the relations of the State to the individual are even now in due process of evolution.

It is the object of this concluding chapter to show, that the Socialist conception, if rightly understood, is not necessarily antagonistic, either to Economic Science or to the State—that, on the contrary, if permitted a peaceful growth, Socialism will increase the number both of good citizens and of intelligent Professors—a consummation much to be desired.

At present the State is everywhere seen to resent strongly the new pressure from below, and gives, when it does give, with no good grace; the demands made upon it are frequently ill-defined and frequently also dishonest. The Vessel of State appears to those on board to be asked to undertake some voyage for the discovery of another continent; no pilot is on the ship, nor any completed chart of the ocean. So that the immense social forces which have evidently broken loose, and which appeal so strongly to the sympathies and the imagination of men, are at present worse than wasted forces; they are as cyclones, they impede progress, they have evaded Eolus and are chasing one another about the Universe, true demons of terror and discord. Thus it happens that because absurdities are being demanded by the fanatical few, the State is in danger of coming into conflict with the expectant many; because unable to do everything, the State would be inclined to do nothing if only it were possible to bury Socialism under a handful of old school-books.

Voltaire has somewhere said that "the art of Government is to make two-thirds of a nation pay all it possibly can pay, for the benefit of the other third," but this is ceasing to be true or possible. In England we have recently deprived the capitalist middle classes of the political control which for many years had been theirs, by adding to the electorate an immense body of men who have everything to gain, and little to lose by any extension of the functions of the State. It is certain therefore that the State will be required in the future to largely extend the sphere of its duties, and it only remains to decide what are those duties which the State can undertake with the least probability of disaster, and with the best prospect of satisfactory results. At the outset of this inquiry it may be assumed that the State is in a position to recognize without any discussion the distinction between the Socialist demands which it must refuse and those demands which it may fairly consider. There is a demand on the part of a very few that wealth already created and which has become private property should be redistributed, whether by positive confiscation or by excessive taxation; this is the red spectre of "the International,"[1] a form of Socialism quite anti-social and which it is not my intention to discuss; but the Socialism which is to-day entitled to a fair consideration is that which demands the employment of the machinery of the State, to ensure a less faulty distribution of the future wealth which is destined to be created from time to time.

What then are those functions which the State can discharge more cheaply and more efficiently than private enterprise, and is it possible so to generalize, that without a series of dangerous and costly experiments, the State may recognize in advance what these functions are? This is the problem which the rulers of the western nations will shortly be required to consider.

Among other successful experiments in State intervention, we have for our guidance the example of the post-office. Here is a department which in the hands of the State has safe-guarded the community against such a collapse as, always

[1] See M. Emile de Laveleye's work, *Socialism of To-day*.

possible in the case of private enterprise, would paralyze at least for a time the whole industrial body. Yet the post-office, though remarkably successful, is a clear infraction of the economic dogma of *laissez faire;* if A had been permitted to contract to deliver all letters in Middlesex and B in Surrey, it is certain that a penny postage rate would have never been heard of, that the four millions sterling of annual profit would not now be going to diminish taxes, and not only so, but we should be getting our letters far less regularly and far less rapidly. Here then is the instance of the State using efficiently an enormous machinery which would be beyond the power of individuals to control, and using this machinery to the profit and advantage of the community; it is the instance of an immense centralized administration of the greatest possible advantage. The State having become in this instance an efficient distributor, is it not probable that other operations of the middle-man can be similarly undertaken, so that while the community might get the advantage of lower prices, the State may collect a great portion or even the whole of its revenue solely from its own economy of system in connecting the Producer with the Consumer? Indeed, is it not possible that because the democracy has, under our extended franchise, now displaced the middle classes—the classes dominated by the middle-man—the demand made by the democracy is really this—that while the domain of Production shall still belong entirely to the individual, so that effort and individuality may not be impaired, yet the distribution of Products shall be left in a degree definable by moral science to the direct intervention of the State? is it not probable that the concern of political parties, or at least of a future political party, will be to effect such an evolution of Economic Science, at present most incomplete, that it may be made to satisfy the requirements of a Scientific Socialism? It is the present grievance of the masses everywhere that the State does nothing for them; its machinery is being entirely employed to advance the interests of the middle and upper classes. What concern has the proletariat in the cheapness of telegrams which it never receives, or in cheap postal connections which it never uses! It is little wonder then that to the masses of the community the State appears at best as a cynical spectator of their wretchedness, only now and then waking up to the necessity of sending its policemen to break a few heads. If in the future the State can be associated in the minds of these classes with any operations by which their daily needs are supplied more cheaply and more effectually, if the State is seen to be both the largest and the most considerate employer of their labour, something of the mutuality of those interests which originally brought Society together will be again diffused, within the lines of a wider sympathy.

And the State having proved itself such an efficient middle-man in distributing letters and telegrams, there is a far larger machinery of distribution ready to its hand, in the Railway System of the country. The present direction of the demand is that the State shall merely interfere to decide freight rates—an interference of the same mischievous nature as that which in the case of Irish land has been attended by disaster and discord. The right of the State to buy what it requires has come to be generally admitted, but interference—without purchase—with vested rights has always resulted, and must always result, in a feeling of insecurity, and such a consequent reduction of values as must injure all parties in the State.

It seems nearly certain that the State ownership of Railroads would, economically considered, be at least as advantageous as has been the case with the Postal and Telegraph systems, and it is most reasonable that these roads, which are the very arteries of the commerce of the various countries, should be operated not as at present, to fill the pockets of a handful of shareholders, but to support and stimulate National industries, for the greatest happiness of the greatest number. Just as was the case with the penny postal rate and the sixpenny telegram, where the initial losses in consequence of the reduction of rates were on such a scale that a mere body of shareholders would never have permitted so costly an experiment, so with the railways to-day; probably if a third-class ticket from London to Edinburgh cost five shillings instead of thirty-five, after a few months or years the diminished charge would have so increased the volume of travel, that the community would be, as it were, making money at both ends—would be travelling at a seventh of the present cost, and the Railways would be paying, just as the Post Office does, a growing proportion of the required Revenue. Two years since I was discussing with the freight manager of an American Railway a "war of rates" at that time active between Chicago and the Pacific Ocean! Railway tickets were being issued from San Francisco to Chicago and back—some 4800 miles—for £3 instead of the usual £30; the result was such an increase of travel that the Western Companies were obliged to borrow rolling stock from the Eastern roads, and the trains were running out of San Francisco daily, quite full—sixty passengers in each long passenger coach. And low though the fares were, it soon appeared that at nine hundred dollars per coach for the "round trip" the railways were at least not losing money, while the business in the local towns, in Ogden, Salt Lake City, in Denver and Omaha, was much increased; within a few weeks, however, the war came to an end, and the old scale of fares was restored, to the great loss of the community, to the no very considerable gain even of the railway companies, but to the immense relief of their employés, upon whom the strain of the increased work had come. It is quite certain that if the railways of the United States are eventually to become the property of the Government, the constituents will at once secure that fares are reduced at least two-thirds, even though at present, if regarded from the standpoint of private enterprises, American railway charges are exceptionally moderate. The amount of capital involved in such a purchase operation would be very large: in England some eight hundred millions, in the United States more than twice as much; but, as a matter of fact, it would be largely a refunding operation; the present holders of bonds and shares, who are perhaps getting four per cent., would be certain, if bought out by a Government issue of consols, to reinvest at three per cent. or less in the new Government Stock; a three per cent. Government, secured Stock, irredeemable for fifty years and clear of all possible Stock Exchange manipulation, would have at least as high a market value as a four per cent. Company Stock. Instead then of half a hundred railway companies, each with a staff more or less efficient, and amateur directors more or less useful and wasteful, and the present costly competition between empty express trains, at the direct expense of third-class travellers by the slower trains, there would be, as is the case in Prussia, Italy, and Belgium, a Government Department which would include the most skilful specialist talent in the country, at high salaries. Of course there would come a howl from Wall Street and the Stock Exchange, for it would no longer be possible for syndicates and railway kings to manipulate Stocks, and by "bull" and "bear" raids, and by fictitious intelligence affecting the prices of securities, to keep the community and the interests of the *bonâ fide* invester in a perpetual state of unrest. A single firm of brokers, selling a single Government Stock, at a price as free from variations as consols are, could do the work now done by a hundred firms; and although this collapse of speculation would involve a loss to some brokers and middle-men, it is evident that their losses would be recouped ten times over by the general community.[1]

In the United States the time for such a development as this is most opportune. That nation is very anxious to continue its present protective Tariff, because, relieved from the free competition of other countries where the labourer is constrained to work far longer hours, the American working-man looks confidently forward to a working day restricted to six hours; but the present difficulty is this—how, without increasing the competition of the foreigner by Tariff

---

[1] Messrs. Chapman and Hall have published recently a book by the late Mr. Charles Waring, the eminent railway contractor, upon the *State Purchase of Railways*, in which the case for Reform is stated with much ability. The views advanced by the late Mr. Waring are the more important, as coming from one who to much distinction in the field of economic science added that further claim to the attention of the community which results from a particularly successful business career.

reductions, still to get into circulation the mass of surplus revenue which the Tariff on imported goods continues to accumulate in the Treasuries —on what National undertaking can this surplus be profitably expended. A surplus revenue of more than thirty millions sterling, accumulating year by year, would, after paralyzing prices, in a very few years lock up the entire currency of the country, and bring the nation back again to the sweet simplicity of exchange by barter. But if the National Debt of the United States was increased by the State purchase of the entire Railroad System, not one dollar of this surplus revenue need ever linger in the Treasury; the fares on the railways might be reduced to such an extent that labour could migrate at the minimum of cost to those centres, whether in the west or south, where any temporary and active demand for labour should spring up, and in return for the Tariff collected in the ports—a Tariff levied largely on the luxuries of the rich—the necessaries of a cheaper subsistence for the working classes could be brought at an ever diminishing cost from the prairie areas west of the Mississippi river. Thus because exports and production also, in consequence of the lower freight charges, would increase, imports, and therefore the revenue collected on imported goods, would also increase; in fifty years by such means the entire railways of the United States might be bought up, paid for, and made a present to the community. Were the railways once in the hands of the State it might be a sound National Policy to carry all third-class passengers everywhere free, and to reduce the freight charges to the mere cost of operating the railroads, leaving the interest charges required by the purchasing operation to be paid for out of the Tariff Revenue, and out of the increased value of the assets of the capitalists of the community; these assets necessarily appreciating *pari passu* with the reduction in transit charges. Such a condition of things would so stimulate emigration from Europe to America that it would be wise and even necessary to pick and to choose—to admit only those emigrants who were able to secure the certificate of the parish priest and doctor, endorsed by the Consul; under such conditions the moral and physical supremacy of the United States citizen of the future would be assured. Is not such a conception of the dignity and the future of the Great Republic more worthy of its position than any mere peddling reduction of the Tariff on imports, which both political parties profess to deprecate in the interests of the working man, because the change must involve a fall of wages, and the underselling of American labour in American markets by the competition of the toiling, overstrained producers of Germany, where men and women also are at their handicrafts seven days in the week.

And while it appears to be to the general interest, in every fairly developed country, that the railways shall come into possession of the community, in the United States this offers the only prospect of protecting the citizens from the tyranny of "Rings" and "Trusts"; there is no other country in the world where the equitable distribution of wealth is being so tampered with by organizations of millionnaire middle-men who, possessing the monopoly of certain markets, have suppressed all competition, and are able both to buy from the producer at a price which they dictate, and also to force the consumer to purchase at monopoly prices. These Rings have become so suddenly and so colossally wealthy, that nothing short of State intervention will avail to protect the community. There is the Standard Oil Company, which controls the entire production and sale of mineral oils in the United States. The monopoly of Messrs. Armour and Swift, the "Butcher

Kings" of Chicago, who are able to dictate the price of beef, mutton, and pork in all the towns of New England and New York. There is a "Sugar Trust," which has either closed or is to-day controlling all the sugar refineries in the United States; there is a "Milk Trust," and also a "Whiskey Ring"; while a combination of the Ice Companies last summer raised the price of ice suddenly some three hundred per cent. This tyranny of Produce "Rings," though at present but a few years old, is rapidly extending, and it is only possible to control it by putting the principal machinery of distribution—the Railways—into the power of the State. If deprived of this machinery, the operations of these "Rings" would be impossible, and a tyranny which is assuming immense proportions, and which is a prodigy of skilful organization, would come to an end for ever.

Of no less importance to the welfare of the community than the ownership of the Railways would be the State purchase of Banks, and the consequent control of the Great Money Power, which is to-day all over the world deciding, without any reference to national interests or national liberties, the issues of peace and war. It is not too much to affirm, that not only is the

Money Power dominating the legislatures, but it is in the sight of all men aggravating by process of legislation the burden of all debt, whether national or private, for the benefit of a few overpowerful creditors. It may, indeed, be affirmed, without fear of contradiction, that legislation arranged in the interest of a certain class, first by Lord Liverpool in this country, and again by Sir Robert Peel at the instigation of Mr. Jones Loyd and other wealthy bankers, which was supplemented recently by simultaneous anti-silver legislation in Berlin and Washington at the instance of the great financial Houses—this legislation has about doubled the burden of all National Debts by an artificial enhancement of the value of money. The fall of all prices induced by this cause has been on such a scale, that while in twenty years the National Debt of the United States quoted in dollars has been reduced by nearly two-thirds, yet the value of the remaining one-third, measured in wheat, in bar iron, or bales of cotton, is considerably greater— is a greater demand draft on the labour and industry of the nation than was the whole debt at the time it was contracted.[1] The aggravation of

[1] See Article, 'Gold Scarcity,' *Nineteenth Century Review*, Oct. 1885.

the burdens of taxation induced by this so-called "appreciation of gold," which is no natural appreciation, but has been brought about by class legislation to increase the value of the gold which is in a few hands, requires but to be explained to an enfranchised Democracy, which will know how to protect itself against further attempts to contract the currency and to force down prices, to the confusion of every existing contract.

Of all classes of middle-men, bankers have been by far the most successful in intercepting and appropriating an undue share of produced wealth. While the modern system of Banking and Credit may be said to be even yet in its infancy, that portion of the assets of the community which is to-day in the strong boxes of the Bankers would, if declared, be an astounding revelation of the recent profits of this particular business; and not only has the business itself become a most profitable monopoly, but its interests in a very few hands are diametrically opposed to the general interests of the majority. By legislation intended to contract the currency and force down all prices, including wages, the price paid for labour, the money owner has been able to increase the purchase power of his sovereign or dollar by the direct diminution of the price of every kind of property measured in money. The monopoly of banking should therefore be acquired by the State; if left to individuals the temptation to arrange such legislation as will contract the currency and increase the value of the standard money is too great. Even were the State unwise enough to abuse its powers, then these enormous profits would in the form of Revenue, at least inure to the benefit of the community. Nearly twenty years ago, and at a time when gold was *depreciating*, Bagehot published the following table of the result of his inquiry into the profits of 110 British Banks whose annual statements he had examined.

NO. OF COMPANIES.	CAPITAL.	DECLARED DIVIDENDS.
15	£ 5,302,767	Above 20 per cent.
20	£ 5,439,439	Between 15 and 20 per cent.
36	£14,056,950	Between 10 and 15 per cent.
36	£14,182,379	Between 5 and 10 per cent.
3	£ 1,350,000	Under 5 per cent.
Total 110	£40,331,535	

As may be seen from the present returns of the four leading London Banks, these profits have been more than maintained, notwithstanding the extreme depression of trade which has characterized the past fifteen years.

NO. OF SHARES.	NAME.	LAST ANNUAL DIVIDEND.	AMOUNT PAID UP ON EACH SHARE.	PRESENT SELLING PRICE OF SHARES.
140,000	Lond. & Westmr.	$15\frac{1}{2}$	20	66
120,000	Lond. Jt. Stock	$12\frac{1}{2}$	15	38
110,000	Union Bk. Lond.	$12\frac{1}{2}$	$15\frac{1}{2}$	39
40,000 / 150,625	Natl. Prov. Bank.	19	$10\frac{1}{2}$ / 12	45 / 52

The capital of these Banks is more than forty-nine millions sterling, of which £8,607,500 has been called up. The shares represented by this sum at their selling price to-day would realize £27,722,500, a profit of over two hundred per cent. It is clear that if banking is to continue to be even as profitable as at present, its monopoly in the hands of the State would result in the rapid redemption of the National Debt. It is evident also from the phenomenal success of the Joint Stock Banks operated by salaried managers, that banking is pre-eminently a business which could be conducted by a State department, neither less profitably nor less safely than as at present. There is no reason why, for example, Mr. Astle, the Manager of the London and Westminster Bank, should look less closely into the credit of individuals, if he were responsible to a Secretary of State, instead of as now to a Board of Directors which meets once a month. As things are banking is in no sense "free"; on the contrary Banks are so restricted by State regulations that, as Professor Bonamy Price remarks of the Bank of England—" It is a self-acting institution of the State working on the Bank's premises, and directed by rules laid down by the State, and absolutely beyond the control of the Bank Directors." Where the State can afford to meddle the State can better still afford to buy. The Banks are a case in point. Individuality is not only of no value in banking, but it is probably an element of risk; and if this is so, if there is a business dangerous to the interests of the community, which on many occasions in modern history has controlled the executive and tampered with the legislatures, and which is excessively profitable, is there any reason why it should not become even as the Post Office, a State monopoly equally valuable to every class of the community? The present law, " Peel's Act " of 1844, by which the State agrees to meddle with monetary legislation whenever it thinks fit, has hardly one disinterested advocate at the present time. It is generally supposed that Sir Robert Peel permitted Mr. Samuel Jones Loyd to draft the entire Bill, which to this day continues unrepealed. It was a Bill intended to deliver over the community tied and bound into the hands of their bankers at every recurring time of crisis. By the present Act, the Act of 1844, the State is virtually made to say this—"There are recurring times of money panics—Black Fridays. At such times early arrivals will be able to borrow from the bankers, but at enormous rates, others will come too late to borrow at all; the more intense the crisis the more intense also the general sufferings. We shall, however, always permit these sufferings to go to that extreme length where, individuals having been ruined wholesale, the general solvency of the Banks themselves has in turn become endangered; at that moment we will intervene, and by suspending the Act terminate the crisis." And seeing that such State intervention in the case of a State so wealthy as Great Britain must always terminate a crisis, it would be equally efficacious to prevent any tendency to a crisis. In other words, were the State the banker, the community would be protected against the recurrence of calamities by which, while one man is making a sovereign, ten men by the collapse of business and the general unsettlement of values are losing ten sovereigns.

There is a letter from Lord George Bentinck written during the money panic of 1847,[1] and

[1] Dated November 3rd, 1847.

which is published in the Croker correspondence. Lord George writes :—

The Act was conditionally suspended last Monday week. The week previous a manufacturer holding £100,000 North-Western Railway debentures (guaranteed five per cent. for five years) required bank-notes to meet his liabilities. He went to Samuel Jones Loyd, and desired to have his debentures discounted. Samuel Jones Loyd refused. The manufacturer replied, "I must have money." The banker rejoined, "I can't do it. But stay—strike off 25 per cent. and I will; but I give but five minutes to consider." The wretched manufacturer had no choice but to submit to the extortion or to suspend payments. Samuel Jones Loyd gave £75,000 Bank of England notes, and became possessed of £100,000 North-Western Railway debentures. On the Monday following—the restrictions of the Bank Charter Act being suspended, the Bank of England was set at liberty to discount such a security at eight per cent. for three months. Jones Loyd consequently on the Monday could have gone to the Bank of England and have rediscounted for £2000 what he himself four days before extorted £25,000 for discounting. Is not usury like this enough to make one's blood boil? Peel's monetary laws must be broken down, or the landed property of the country, burdened with encumbrances, will pass into the hands of the Christian Jews.

It is unnecessary to multiply instances of the injurious working of the present monetary legislation; if it was intended merely to pile up the few mammoth fortunes of this generation at the expense of the general industries, it has certainly achieved its end.

The Socialist proposals of Mr. Henry George and others, that the State shall become the universal landlord, appear to be both uneconomical and even unattractive. If the State is to become an owner, it requires to buy what is at present profitable, not what is becoming fitfully more and more profitless. To nationalize land under present conditions would be to nationalize pauperism; the evil is in this, that owing to an increasing redundancy of middle-men, and the profits of middle-men, the general producer is being ruined. It is therefore essential so to arrange it that the owners of the instruments of production, especially of the soil, the "nursing mother" of us all, shall be secured a full share of profit. As M. Thiers once finely expressed it, " A peasant in every homestead, in every hand a gun, for the defence of property and of our liberties; " and this consummation of conservative socialism is quite impossible unless some cheaper method of distribution can be arranged which, while reducing prices to the consumer, will yet leave a larger profit to the producer. Visions of nationalizing the land, and of the establishment of a peasant proprietary, are mere phantoms until the cultivator has been enabled to obtain much more nearly the present retail prices paid by the consumer for what the cultivator produces; it is the sorely-tried producer whom we are concerned to assist, and the assistance will have to be afforded not at the expense of the consumer, but at the expense of the middle-man. This can only be secured by the direct agency of the State; and when a large proportion of the middle-men distributors have reverted to the producing classes, so that production tends to increase; then it may be possible to satisfy also a further socialist demand—the reduction of the hours of labour by legislation.

But now I hear it said, "Granted that the State can distribute much more cheaply than the individual, so that one broker or one commission man can do the work now done by ten, what then is to happen to the nine?" But when the franchise now in the hands of the working classes —the classes especially concerned that while production shall be profitable, the consumption price shall be low—when this franchise was the prerogative of the middle classes, the reply to exactly the same question, when asked by the agricultural classes whose occupation was being taken away from them, was, "Emigrate." Free Trade was to make of England the *entrepôt* of the world— one monstrous middle-man, commission agent, broker, banker; the Political Economy then devised with much scientific assurance was a bullet-proof process-server, and the nation was required to recognize the governing policy of "Manacles or Manitoba," as a yoke which had been in readiness since the beginning of the world, to be fitted in the nineteenth century upon the patient neck of labour. But now the old order changes, and in the fulness of time the power with the franchise has come into other hands; by comparison with the hardships inflicted upon these working men, who, with no capital and little education, were told to "move on" over great seas in the steerage quarters of a sailing ship, or failing that to starve at home, it is a small thing to say to certain middle-men, for the most part capitalists, "London is to-day nearer to Montreal than seventy years since it was to Edinburgh; therefore emigrate freely to the colonies, where your education and your capital will secure you a proper welcome; you must yield the field to a more economical process of distribution which will remedy some of the present awful inequalities of social conditions."

How far such a re-arrangement can be profitably extended is the problem of future politics. How and where the line can be drawn between the province of the Individual—Production, the province of the State—Distribution,—these things are in the lap of the gods, the gods perhaps of the political gallery; whether the same cart which delivers our letters may be destined also to distribute loaves and legs of mutton,—such considerations as these are far beyond the present field of political preparedness. Suffice to say, that the larger the State domain the better for the workers. Industrial individualism is to-day a ruthless employer, the young to the Mill, the old to the workhouse; whereas the State, in the distributing departments connected with its railways, will be able to find suitable light employment at fair wages for thousands of the old and enfeebled who now become a burden on the rates.

But without suggesting that it is the future function of the State to become the "Universal Provider," it is pretty evident that the system of Limited Liability Companies has done more harm than good, that whenever Joint Stock Companies can be profitably operated, the State could be more successful than they; and wherever Joint Stock Companies, as in the majority of instances, are expensive failures competing on ruinous terms with private enterprise, and profitable not to the public, but to certain brokers and commission agents, it is time their operations should be suppressed. Bagehot declares that the Joint Stock principle is only successfully applicable in cases where (1) The capital is not used to work the business, but to guarantee the business; or (2) where Companies have an exclusive privilege; or (3) where they have undertaken a business both large and simple, employing more money than most individuals have at command, and yet such that, in Adam Smith's words, "the operations are capable of being reduced to a routine, or such an uniformity of method as admits of no variation."

These are the three conditions which Bagehot held to cover the profitable operations of the Joint Stock principle; the first includes Banks and Insurance Companies, the second Patents, the third Railways. Not only can the State cover the entire field, but by assuming monopoly rights, as it has done in the case of the

Post Office and Telegraph, it can almost indefinitely extend its domain of "exclusive privilege." An attempt has recently been made by Prince Bismarck in Germany to inaugurate State Insurance Companies, the profits of which are intended to secure to working men a sustentation fund against their old age. If the great Chancellor had before him the returns of the entire list of English Insurance Companies, fifty-six in number—the good, the bad, and the indifferent —it is not surprising that he should have recognized in this direction a brightened future for the labouring classes. These fifty-six companies last year paid an average of over eighteen per cent. in dividends! One of the largest Companies, the Union Assurance, paid a dividend of 120 per cent, and its £20 shares are selling for £550. In view of such results as these, it may be safely affirmed, that had the Railways, the Banks, and the Insurance Companies been operated for the last fifty years by the State, while the community might probably have been served better and more cheaply, our National Debt could have been redeemed out of the "unearned increment," and the revenue now required in this country to carry on the Government could be supplied from year to year by the surplus profits earned in these three departments alone. There is the promise that the "eternal fitness of things" may be herein exemplified. Let us look a little closer. The profits of Banks and Insurance Companies are in proportion to the goodness of their credit. How much stronger is not the credit of the State than that of the corporation? And the credit of the State has itself been secured by past and present generations of those who make up the State—in other words, by the continued patience of the tax-payers. That form of modern credit therefore which is exemplified so strikingly by the earnings of Banks and Insurance Companies, and is farmed now by a mere handful of individuals, is yet closely connected with the credit of the State, which credit has been earned, and should therefore be enjoyed by, the citizens in its material, and not merely moral equivalent. And this being so, is not this faith justified—that all unconsciously the State has been doing its duty, and respecting its pledges in order that in due time its vast modern machinery could be constructed and operated, not at the expense of the tax-payers, but directly out of the profits of the Public Credit.

It remains to consider the objections to the

State Distribution of Products—a form of Socialism which will necessarily meet with the organized opposition of the middle classes everywhere. It may be conceded, that so colossal an increase of the State patronage would immensely strengthen the position of the Government of the day as against the Opposition. Hundreds of thousands of Government employés, whose employment might, theoretically, be held to depend upon the continuance of a party in power, would bring an immense support to the Government at elections. But Democracies are fickle and impulsive, and it is possible that if we in England are to avoid such political distractions as are now in France driving out one Ministry after another, that then an immense unshifting ballast, which would be afforded by the employés of the State, is the best remedy which can be devised. And, too, the more extensive the system of patronage and employment, the less the possibility of its abuse; it would be impossible, in the event of a change of Government, for the in-coming Ministers to turn out, for example, all the postmen, all the railway porters, still less all the bank officials. It could not be done; the country would not permit its business to suffer by any such wholesale evictions, and to remove merely the heads of departments would not in these days of secret voting affect the fortune of the war. It is probable also that a majority of the community, both in England and the United States, would welcome any changes which added largely to the stability and permanence of any Government. These communities generally have never shared in the excitement which the chief actors themselves derive from rapid political changes, and would gladly avoid such visitations as frequent elections, which periodically unsettle all business.

It may still be objected that at least in England there is nothing in the present condition of the great State departments which would justify the nation in extending the State functions. But this, though a strong argument for reforms in the spending departments, is no argument at all against the probability of good results in certain earning departments. Because the War Office is found to be uneconomical and incomplete, no one proposes to abolish the Post Office. And from the fact that the German War Office is so nearly perfect, it is clear that what we are complaining of is not the inefficiency of State control generally, but merely of a particular system, which appears to have survived its utilities.

Of course the older Professors will still cleave to their dogmas of *laissez faire*, and deprecate any extension of the State function; but their academic principles have already disappeared from the practices of modern legislation, and the common sense, at least of the Anglo-Saxon peoples, has always looked upon the rather pedantic objection to any increase of State agency as a mere metaphysical dissertation, applying not only to the extension of Government, but also about as logically to the principle of any Government and of any society at all. While the Professors have been educating us to appreciate the propriety of a vast legislative centralization, the demand for Home Rule has been springing up in all parts of the world; and while also the importance of keeping the State altogether outside of any industrial co-operation such as might lead to real cheapness is still the text of every lecture, we are experiencing the rapid spread of a belief in both the economy and the capacity of State agency.

If this then is the form of Socialism for which the world is getting ready, there is nothing very terrible a-head, and our coming revolution may well be a bloodless one. For these are concessions which the State may fairly grant; and just as the process of inoculation should properly precede the outbreak of epidemic, so the wisdom of the State will be shown in proportion as these concessions are granted in time. Nor should it be lost sight of, that to political parties will be supplied a distinct issue, which will keep them from breaking up over mere side issues into disordered and shifting sections, and this to-day is a matter of the first importance. There is that in every man which will intuitively decide for him whether he belongs to the Party of Socialism, or whether the principle of Individualism which has been asserted so gallantly and so usefully by the master minds both of this century and the last, is even yet more valuable to direct our legislation than any benefits which might result from the more extended agency of the State.

The world has become the theatre of a new struggle—the struggle of the enfranchised masses to secure certain concessions from the classes— the middle classes. There are not wanting the symptoms that in this struggle the aristocracy, their interests being coincident, will be found ranged on the side of the people.

The conflict is inevitable. Privileges wrested from the Church by the Throne, from the Throne by the Aristocracy, have in turn come within the control of the Middle Classes. On the whole, these have used their powers worthily and well. But recently they have permitted the power to be absorbed by a mere section of their body— a non-producing section of extreme intelligence and capacity.

It is hardly probable that the social struggles of nine hundred years can have culminated in the enduring conquest of that class which is to-day battening alike upon the producer and the consumer.

APPENDIX.

THE ECONOMIC DISTURBANCES SINCE 1873.

Reprinted from THE COMMERCIAL AND FINANCIAL CHRONICLE
(*New York*).

COMMERCIAL depression may result from two distinct causes, either over-investment of capital, involving increase in the supply of goods and change in the methods of production; or contraction of currency and credit, involving decrease in the available means of exchange. The crisis of 1857 was an example of the latter; that of 1847 in England furnished a good instance of the former.

It is only in their beginnings that the two causes are distinct. As matters progress, each becomes complicated with the other. Over-production produces a fall in prices, loss of credit, and mercantile failures; and thereby lessens the facilities for payment, exactly as if there had been contraction of currency. Contraction of currency, on the other hand, reduces the immediate purchasing power of the community, and leaves producers and middle-men with unsold goods on their hands, exactly as if there had been an over-production of those goods. The state of things in the advanced stages of a commercial crisis can often be explained on either cause indiscriminately according to the personal bias of the investigator. Until recently the tendency of most writers was to lay too much stress on matters of banking and currency, and too little on changes in the method of production. The majority of practical English economists of the last generation had gained their chief experience in banking, and had little or no knowledge of manufacturing business. It was natural that they should exaggerate the importance of the causes which came under their own immediate observation. To-day the mistake of these economists is clearly perceived. It is felt that new methods of production are an important cause of commercial crises ; and some people are inclined to regard them as the only cause. In the reaction against the English theory, which treated commercial crises as " panics " of greater or less duration, many writers have gone to the other extreme of considering the contraction as a mere incident, of secondary importance, perhaps more apparent than real, and certainly not an independent factor in the trouble. This is substantially the ground taken by Mr. Wells in an able and carefully-written series of articles on the Economic Disturbances since 1873, which have appeared in the " Popular Science Monthly," and are about to be published in book form. The weight which the writer's name carries and the number of facts which he adduces in support of his conclusions make it important to examine them in detail, and to point out clearly where the argument is open to attack.

CHARACTERISTICS OF THE PRESENT DEPRESSION.

The present crisis is in some respects different from any of its predecessors, because the fall in prices has lasted so long. It is this continuous depression of prices which has stood in the way of any real recovery, and which has made even the active speculations of 1880 and 1881 seem like a mere pause in the descent. To determine the reason why prices have so long continued to fall, is the most important problem in economic science at the present day. But its solution is attended with special difficulties. If the condi-

APPENDIX.—ECONOMIC DISTURBANCES. 167

tions of production had changed while the world's currency system remained the same, we should have one explanation. If the currency system had changed while the conditions of production remained the same, we should have another. But the conditions of production and the world's currency system have both changed at the same time, each in a way which has had no exact parallel in past history; and it becomes an exceedingly delicate matter to determine the relative importance of two causes which so closely inter-act with one another.

The problem has a practical as well as a speculative interest. If the crisis is simply due to improvements in production, we have nothing to do but to wait for these things to work out their own result. It may be long and hopeless waiting, but we could not expect to turn back and resist the progress of invention in the industrial world any more than the trades unionist can expect to resist for any length of time the introduction of machinery in his particular trade. But if the crisis is to any considerable degree due to the demonetization of silver, the case at once assumes a different aspect. It becomes a matter with which Governments may have at once the power and the duty to interfere.

Mr. Wells tries to exclude the latter cause altogether. He holds, first, that the general fall in prices, such as it is, is amply accounted for by man's increased control over the productive forces of nature; and, second, that if we examine the history of individual articles, we shall find reasons for the lower prices of most of them in changed conditions of production, while those whose conditions of production have not changed have not fallen in price. We shall examine these propositions in order, considering this week the general effect of improvements in production, and reserving the detailed analysis of prices for subsequent issues.

The effect of improvements generally is to throw an increased quantity of goods on the market at a reduced cost per unit of product. But in anything like a healthful condition of industry, the quantity marketed will increase more rapidly than the price falls. In other words, the aggregate product after the improvement, measured in dollars and cents, should be greater than before. If other things remain exactly the same, this increase in the volume of business will create a need for more money with which to transact it. The old demand for money "to move the crops" had a basis of fact, however wrong the measures may have been by which the United States Treasury undertook to meet it.

Now, no one would deny that there has been an increase in the volume of business in the last twenty years without a correspondingly large increase in the available amount of metallic currency. Either the credit system must have expanded to meet it, or there must have been a virtual contraction of the currency as compared with the wants of trade. It has been the custom to assume that the credit system expands, almost automatically, and that an increasing proportion of business is done without the use of cash. Mr. Wells himself makes this assumption, without trying to prove it. That an increasing *amount* of business is settled without the use of cash, we are ready to admit; that an increasing *proportion* of business is thus settled, we do not believe. The use of cash payments in the retail trade has grown enormously in the last twenty years. At the beginning of that time weekly payment of operatives was exceptional, and various forms of truck or store orders were common. To-day a large proportion of the operatives receive cash weekly from their employers and pay the stores cash down. The same general movement has been going on in the dealings between producers and middle-men. In the ordinary operations of life the tendency to shorten the term of credit has been all but universal. One of the ablest living English economists has boldly challenged the doctrine that, as civilization advances, credit takes the place of money. On the contrary, money takes the place of credit. To see the credit system in its full vigour one must go to half-civilized countries like Turkey. As a country advances it uses more cash.

RELATIVE SCARCITY OF GOLD ADMITTED.

But if volume of business and use of cash are both increasing, it follows of necessity that a failure to increase the supply of metallic money involves a relative scarcity of means of payment. Mr. Wells in one place incidentally admits this, and seems to think it an unimportant admission. But it really involves giving up his whole case. It is precisely this relative scarcity which makes the trouble. The Suez Canal, and the railroads, and the other improvements in transportation, on which Mr. Wells lays so much stress, are means of lessening the price to consumers; but that is not the difficulty. The difficulty is that something else comes in and lowers the price to the producers; and there is a strong *prima facie* reason to believe that it is something connected with the currency. Mr. Wells tries to make improvements account for too much. Reduced rates from Chicago to Liverpool will account for lower prices at Liverpool; but they will not account for lower prices at Chicago. The introduction of a new machine may account for commercial distress among the owners of the old machines, but it will not explain why this distress should be shared by the owners of the new one.

Mr. Wells says, in brief, that improvements have reduced cost of production, and that therefore prices have fallen. We do not dispute this. But we deny that it is a complete explanation of the facts before us. Improvements have also increased the volume of business. The world's available currency has not been allowed to increase correspondingly in volume. A relative contraction has been thus caused which has made it more difficult to carry on the world's trade, and which has given rise to the existing distress among producers—a distress too widespread and too profound to be fully explained by Mr. Wells' methods.

As long as Mr. Wells confines himself to generalities concerning man's increased control over the productive forces of nature, or to remote causes like the Suez Canal, it is hardly necessary to answer him. But when he attempts to explain why particular commodities have fallen and are falling in price, he touches matters which are more important and more easy to decide. We believe that many of his conclusions are wrong simply because many of his facts are wrong.

MR. WELLS' STATEMENTS AS TO WHEAT.

Take, for instance, those relating to wheat. Of all the articles in his list this is probably the one whose fall in price has had most to do with the distinctive features of the present crisis. Wheat in England has fallen to less than two-thirds of its former figures. In the United States the decline has been hardly less marked. There has been some decrease in cost of production, but nothing corresponding to this. How does Mr. Wells explain it? "An all-sufficient explanation," he says, "would seem to be found in the circumstance that all investigation shows that the comparatively recent increase in the world's supply of food has been greatly in excess of the concurrent increase of the world's population." This is a sweeping statement, and one which we cannot accept. We do not know of any such investigation which has shown anything of the kind. Mr. Wells certainly has not proved it. The evidence which he adduces breaks down completely. Parts of it are palpably untrue or unfair; while those which will stand the test of examination do not prove his proposition, but rather the reverse.

"According to Mr. Neumann-Spallart," he says, "the production of cereals in Europe doubled from 1869 to 1879, and in the case of Russia her exports of wheat increased from 36,565,000 bushels in 1880 to 67,717,000 in 1884." Neumann-Spallart is probably the best authority on the world's grain production anywhere to be found; much too good an authority to make the statement here attributed to him. He never said anything of the kind. The fact that Mr. Wells (who is here blindly following Prof. Laughlin) allows himself to be led into such a statement shows that he is quite unfamiliar with the conditions of wheat-production in Europe. It is not merely a misquotation; it is one which no man who writes on the world's wheat supply ought to make. As for Russia, the year 1880 was the worst there has been for a long time in her wheat harvest. In 1878 she exported over 100,000,000 bushels; so that if Mr. Wells had compared 1884 with 1878 instead of with 1880, he would have found a decrease of 34 millions instead of an increase of 31 millions. The exports of Russian wheat for the five years 1880-1884 were almost exactly the same as for the five years 1876-1880; if anything, a trifle less, in spite of all the increased facilities for putting the crop on the market.

Mr. Wells' statements concerning the United States are hardly less open to attack. "The cereal production of the United States increased from 932,752,000 bushels in 1862 to 2,992,881,000 in 1884; or in the ratio of 452 per cent." It may be remarked that Mr. Wells' arithmetic at this point seems, to say the least, a trifle peculiar; but let that pass. The real objection to this comparison is that the initial year is by no means a fair one. In 1862 little more than half of the country was available either for production or for enumeration; men's best energies were turned to fighting and not to wheat-raising. No wonder that North and South together, in profound peace, and at the end of twenty years of unparalleled growth, should raise three times as much grain as was grown in 1862 by the States then available for enumeration, in the midst of an exhausting war. The only wonder is that Mr. Wells should make the use he does of a comparison so distinctly unfair in its basis.

But he has another set of facts with regard to the United States, which impress him so much that he repeats them twice over. "The average wheat production of the United States for the five years from 1881 to 1885, inclusive, was 436,000,000 bushels; while for the ten years preceding—some of which supplied the heaviest demands for exportation ever experienced—the average was only 366,000,000 bushels." Very true; but what does it prove? One of these periods was, on an average, seven and a half years later than the other. The increase of population in the United States in such a period is more than 20 per cent. To have kept pace with such increase, the wheat product for the second period should have been at least 450 millions instead of 436. Mr. Wells' theory about food supply increasing faster than population falls to the ground, in this instance at any rate. This will be still clearer in tabular form.

	1871-80. Bushels.	1881-85. Bushels.
Average annual product	366,000,000	436,000,000
Average annual export of wheat, and wheat reduced to flour	98,000,000	144,000,000
Balance for home consumption	268,000,000	292,000,000
Mean population for the period, estimated	44,000,000	53,000,000
Wheat consumed at home per head of population	6·1	5·5

No system of deduction for seed, &c., will alter the general character of these ratios. For the United States, at any rate, Mr. Wells' "great increase of food supply, as compared with population," turns out to be a decrease of nearly ten per cent.

It is impossible to make similar tables for Europe with any approach to completeness, the statistics of production of exports and of imports being much more complicated. Enough, however, is known to disprove rash statements concerning the relation of wheat supply to population.

APPENDIX.—ECONOMIC DISTURBANCES. 173

The two most careful and most frequently quoted estimates of the population of Europe in modern times are those of Behm and Wagner in 1874, and Levasseur in 1886. The former gives 300 millions of inhabitants for Europe, and the latter 345 millions. Bnt Levasseur's estimates are habitually rather high; and it is probable that an increase of one per cent. annually would just about cover the actual growth. It certainly cannot be less than three-fourths of one per cent.

Now, in the face of this growth, let us look at the harvest estimates of Neumann-Spallart for Europe, which furnish altogether the best data available. To avoid the error due to individual seasons, good or bad, we take average results for decades. We give the figures in hectolitres of a little less than three bushels each.

AVERAGE ANNUAL EUROPEAN HARVEST.

Hectolitres (1 hectolitre equals $2\frac{5}{8}$ bushels).

	1870-80.	1875-84.	Change per cent.
Wheat	454,000,000	440,800,000	—3
Rye	448,700,000	413,800,000	—8
Barley	227,500,000	230,900,000	+1
Oats	541,800,000	524,200,000	—3
Corn	120,800,000	134,500,000	+11
Other grain	102,900,000	88,800,000	—14
Total	1,895,700,000	1,833,000,000	—3½

This deficit has not yet been made up in Europe itself; at least as far as wheat is concerned. Reducing the figures to bushels, and bringing our comparison down to date, we find the wheat crop of Europe to have been as follows:—

	Bushels.
1870-1880 (Neumann)	1,287,000,000
1875-1884 (Neumann)	1,249,000,000
1883 (Neumann)	1,267,000,000
1884 (Neumann)	1,377,000,000
1885 (U. S. Agricultural Department estimate)	1,204,000,000
1886 (U. S. Agricultural Department estimate)	1,173,000,000
1887 (Vienna Congress estimate)	1,259,000,000
Average 1883-1887	1,256,000,000

The last five years thus show an absolute deficit of 30,000,000 as compared with the wheat harvests of a decade earlier. But if we make allowance for the growth of population during that period, which cannot be considered at less than three-fourths of one per cent. annually, we find an additional allowance of at least 100,000,000 bushels needed, in order to give the same relative supply. The real deficit, as compared with the needs of the people, is 130,000,000. How is this made up? 60,000,000 bushels of it from the United States, whose exports of wheat and wheat-flour have risen from 75,000,000 in 1875 to 135,000,000 in 1885; about 40,000,000 from India, whose present wheat export is almost entirely the creation of the last few years; perhaps 10,000,000 from Australia and New Zealand; not quite 5,000,000 bushels from the Argentine Republic; while in other exporting countries — Canada, Egypt, Algiers, Chili, &c.—the gains and losses nearly balance. Even on this minimum estimate of increase of population the per capita wheat supply of Europe would seem to have diminished in the course of the last ten years.

These figures are probably by no means free from errors. We are inclined to think that Neumann's earlier figure was a little too high, and that there has been no very great diminution in the absolute wheat product of Europe. But they are trustworthy enough to show that there has been no marked change in the proportion between wheat supply and population—certainly none which will account for the actual fall in prices. The picture drawn by Mr. Wells of a market, already overstocked, which India and South America are flooding with an increasing surplus, is a fanciful one. What are the four or five million bushels of the Argentine Republic in a market whose annual variations of supply amount to hundreds of millions? The increase in Indian wheat exports during the last five years, instead of being, as Mr. Wells implies, "continuous and of great magnitude," has been trifling in amount and by no means coutinuous from year to year.

That the wheat market is in one sense overstocked, we admit. The fall in price shows it. But that this is due to any over-production as compared with the needs of consumers, we are disposed to deny. If the statistics which we have quoted (and which are quoted by Mr. Wells himself) mean anything at all, they show that the proportion between wheat supply and population in civilized countries has remained substantially unchanged, while the price of wheat has fallen one-third. The apparent excess of supply in trading centres is to be regarded as a congestion of the market rather than a surplus available for the consumer.

COTTON.

We have shown how inadequate was Mr. Wells' explanation of the fall in the price of wheat, and shall now consider the history of the production and prices of cotton; an article less prominently connected in men's minds with the existing depression, but of even greater importance in the international trade of the country. The behaviour of cotton prices in recent years, though to the general observer less noticeable than that of wheat, has really been no less remarkable. Wheat showed an enormous decline in the face of an undiminished popular need; cotton shows not only a persistent failure to advance, but even a marked tendency to decline in the face of a vastly increased demand for consumption. The smaller decline in the one case is as extraordinary as the greater decline in the other.

Mr. Wells passes over the subject lightly. In his detailed account of price movements, the article which furnishes more than one-fourth of our exports receives but one-fortieth of the total space—less than one-half the attention which is devoted to nitrate of soda. Yet even this brief treatment is by no means free from errors of details. "Comparing 1860 with 1885," he says, "the decline in the price of cotton in the New York market has not been material. The year 1886, however, witnessed a decline to a lower point than has been reached, with one exception, since the year 1855. . . . On the other hand, the increase in the world's supply of cotton in recent years has been very considerable, the American crop increasing from 3,930,000 bales in 1872-73 to 6,575,000 in 1885-86, or 67 per cent.; while the supply of the world for the corresponding period is estimated to have increased from 6,524,000 bales to 8,678,000 bales, or at the rate of about 32 per cent. Such an increase in production would undoubtedly have occasioned a more marked decline in price had it not been for a great and coincident increase in the world's consumption of cotton fabrics; which in turn was undoubtedly in consequence of a material decline in the cost of the same, as the result of improvements in machinery and methods of production."

In regard to these statements we note, first, that the initial year chosen is conspicuously unfair. Prices in 1860 represented the lowest point in the reaction against the speculations of 1856-57, and were also unnaturally depressed by the very large crops of the previous seasons. To properly appreciate the effect on prices of the increased production in the United States, bear in mind further that this country previous to that period had been furnishing almost all the supply of the raw material the world had, and yet with the increase from America there was a concurrent increase from "other countries." Thus it happened that the world's new supply in 1857-58 was 4,037,000 bales —only three times in the history of the trade had it previously reached four million bales—of ordinary weights; in 1858-59 it was 4,785,000 bales; and in 1859-60 it grew to the remarkable total of 5,816,000 bales; and it has been asserted by those best able to judge that nothing but the American war saved our cotton producers from a great disaster. We are therefore obviously justified in saying

APPENDIX.—ECONOMIC DISTURBANCES.

that the initial year chosen by Mr. Wells is conspicuously unfair.

But a second fact that vitiates the comparison is that it is based on quotations in the New York market, and yet (1) the initial year is in ante war times when there was no official market here, reports in the different newspapers often differing widely; and, what is even more faulty, (2) it omits to make reference to or any allowance for a material change of grade by the new classification' which has since the war been adopted. The truth is, the Liverpool market affords the only sure basis of comparison accessible to any investigator desiring to reach correct conclusons. For the purpose of this discussion, and to show how wide apart theories and facts may often get, we reproduce from Mr. Ellison's circulars the highest, lowest, and *average* prices at Liverpool for each season since 1856-57, omitting (because of no present use and our space is limited) the years covered by the American war and those following, when prices continued more or less to be influenced by war conditions.

MIDDLING ORLEANS AT LIVERPOOL.

Season of—	Highest.	Lowest.	Average.
1856-57	9·25d.	6·37d.	7·80d.
1857-58	9·25d.	6·31d.	7·14d.
1858-59	7·38d.	6·75d.	7·03d.
1859-60	7·37d.	5·75d.	6·61d.
1860-61	10·12d.	6·50d.	7·66d.
1861-72	Omitted for reasons stated.		
1872-73	10·50d.	9·00d.	9·65d.
1873-74	9·37d.	8·18d.	8·52d.
1874-75	8·37d.	7·18d.	7·87d.
1875-76	7·37d.	6·00d.	6.62d.
1876-77	7·31d.	6·00d.	6·50d.
1877-78	6·87d.	6·00d.	6·51d.
1878-79	7·31d.	5·25d.	6·26d.
1879-80	7·62d.	6·75d.	7·06d.
1880-81	7·43d.	5·81d.	6·62d.
1881-82	7·37d.	6·43d.	6·87d.
1882-83	7·12d.	5·56d.	5·87d.
1883-84	6·56d.	5·87d.	6·20d.
1884-85	6·25d.	5·56d.	5·87d.
1885-86	5·62d.	4·75d.	5·25d.
1886-87	6·00d.	5·19d.	5·50d.

What further need be said with regard to Mr. Wells' assertion that the decline in cotton has not been material? Even making comparison with his initial year of 1859-60 (which is an unfair starting-point, as we have shown), his assertion is certainly surprising in view of the above results. Look at the yearly averages given—at the earlier date (1859-60), 6·61d. per lb., now 5·50d. per lb. That indicates a loss of $1\frac{1}{10}$d. (say approximately $2\frac{1}{5}$ cents) on every pound of cotton the producer sells—one-sixth of the whole gone, call it 50 millions of dollars. We think no planter or dealer—in fact we are inclined to believe no reader—will be able to agree with Mr. Wells that this is an immaterial loss.

Note further the persistency of the decline in the foregoing averages since 1873, when the anti-silver crusade began. Observe that though not wholly uninterrupted, the decline is continuing, each recovery being followed by a lower dip; and this has taken place when, as we shall presently show, under the influence of supply and demand, an advance ought really to have been recorded. Even as to increased supply we see that Mr. Wells' figures are quite inadequate. He has made his comparison on the basis of number of bales produced, whereas from year to year the average weights differ materially. Following the ordinary method of reducing the bales to an average of 400 lbs., it will be seen that the new supply increased between 1872-73 and 1885-86 (the thirteen years he uses) 50 per cent., instead of 32 per cent., as he states it.

But an error which is far more serious than that is in the explanation of the causes which led to this increase of supply. He implies that the larger production was an independent event, and that the increased demand was a sort of lucky coincidence. Obviously, the effect upon prices would be different according as demand was a cause of the increased supply or not. In the former case we should expect prices to rise; in the latter case they would be likely to fall; but even in that case not so materially as they have fallen, unless the supply kept constantly in advance of consumption, accumulating year by year.

Fortunately we have statistics which are so complete that they enable us to answer this question with confidence. No other trade has such perfect records, and the conclusion they teach is clear. The increased use of cotton was the independent event; the increased supply was produced in order to meet the demand thus created.

One of the most striking things in recent industrial history has been the steady growth in cotton consumption. Beginning in 1868, when the total was slightly under five million bales, it advanced, practically without interruption, until 1882-83, when it amounted to about nine and a half million bales of 400 lbs. each—an increase of over 90 per cent. Then there was a slight drop; but matters soon recovered, and the figures for 1886-87 were 200,000 bales higher than for 1882-83. There is no difficulty in accounting for this immense increase. Mr. Wells himself states the reason in part. Improvements in machinery have reduced the price to the consumer; this reduction in price has greatly increased the quantity which the market will take, even in times of commercial depression. But what Mr. Wells fails to see, is the natural effect which this would have on the price of raw cotton. If other things remained the same, it would make the price rise.

Suppose that the raw material in a certain piece of goods cost 2 cents, and that the expenses of manufacturing were 4 cents, the goods cannot be put on the market below 6 cents. Now, suppose that an improvement in machinery reduces the cost of manufacturing to 3 cents, the goods can now be sold at any price above 5 cents. But this produces an increased demand for the raw material. Even if this demand raised the price of the cotton to $2\frac{1}{4}$ cents, there would still be more consumed under the new system than under the old. The old price gave 2 cents to cotton and

4 to manufacture; the new price gives $2\frac{1}{4}$ cents to cotton and 3 to manufacture. The final cost to the consumer is less, and the quantity taken by the market is greater. Improvements in machinery put the manufacturers in position to demand a larger amount of raw material, even if it be at a slightly higher price; and the natural tendency of such increased demand is to make prices rise.

Now, in the case of cotton there has been such an increased demand, and prices have not risen; in fact, they have fallen materially, as we have seen. The fall has not been wholly uninterrupted, but nearly so. Its extent and regularity are made more distinct if we take long enough periods to escape the more temporary causes of variation. In the following we so divide the yearly averages given above from 1873-74 down to the present time; the periods are five years, except the last, which is but four years.

LIVERPOOL AVERAGE PRICES OF MIDDLING ORLEANS.

1873-74 to 1877-78, both inclusive—average per lb. ... .. 7·20d.
1878-79 to 1882-83, both inclusive—average per lb. ... ... 6·54d.
1883-84 to 1886-87, both inclusive—average per lb. ... ... 5·70d.

These figures point strongly toward an appreciation of gold as the only satisfactory explanation. This presumption, if it is to be met at all, must be met in one of two ways—either by showing that there was an over-production, which more than met the demand, or by proving that there were such important changes in the cost of production as to make prices fall to the extent they have fallen, in spite of this tendency toward increased demand.

The first hypothesis is out of the question. There has been no over-production of cotton. The consumption tends to trench more and more closely upon the limits of the available supply. In our annual crop report, figures were given showing not merely the annual production and consumption, but the stocks carried over from year to year. We find that in October, 1872, after a crop of 6,277,000 bales, the supply carried over, visible and invisible, amounted to 2,453,000 bales. Nor was this unprecedentedly large. For the next five years the supply did not fall below 2,300,000 bales. But in more recent times we find that even after the enormous crop of 1883 (10,408,000 bales), the amount carried over was only 2,405,000, or less than it was in 1872; while in subsequent years it has not reached 2,000,000; and, including the current year, has probably not averaged 1,850,000, of which over 650,000 bales is invisible. In other words, this shows a loss of nearly 600,000 bales since 1883, about all of it in the visible supply, leaving only about 1,200,000 bales in sight (that is, stock in ports and afloat all over the world) for spinners' current takings—a wholly inadequate amount for the free working of the mills, as each summer proves, and every one in the trade knows. Or consider it from another point of view. Compare the years of commercial depression now with those of the preceding period of the same character—we find that the absolute surplus has diminished 20 per cent., that the total crop has increased about 40 per cent., and that the proportion of surplus to total crop has diminished 50 per cent. Whatever such facts mean, they clearly do not mean relative over-production.

With regard to changes in the cost of production, it is harder to get positive evidence. On many plantations it has undoubtedly been reduced. People are learning how to use free labour and intelligent methods of cultivation. Yet it must be remembered that the decisive element in the effect on the price of our agricultural products, is the cost of that part of the supply which is produced at the greatest disadvantage, and it is a question whether the majority of planters are cultivating cotton at any less cost than in 1873. But that inquiry need not be pressed, since the decline in price is so material, and the decline, if any, in cost of production must be so slight, as to make it obvious that the lower cotton quotations cannot be accounted for on the theory of a less expenditure of capital and labour in production.

Mr. Wells says that "the decline in prices of the commodities which have been specified has been so largely due to conditions affecting their supply and demand, that if any or all other causes whatever have contributed to such a result, the influence exerted has not been appreciable." The demand for cotton has increased; the stocks of cotton have diminished; there has been no tendency to over-production, and no radical change in the conditions of supply; at the same time prices between the first and last period given in the above statement have fallen off over one-fifth. Our readers can draw their own conclusions.

We have shown that there has been no real over-production of wheat or cotton. These are the two most important articles in the trade of the United States. A theory which does not explain the price of these articles cannot be accepted as satisfactory.

MEAT.

But wheat and cotton do not stand alone. Mr. Wells' statements concerning many other articles in his list will be found to be misleading. We have neither the space nor the time to enter into a detailed examination of the whole field of industry; it will be sufficient if we point out a few of the most serious errors into which Mr. Wells has fallen.

He mentions as one important factor in the recent fall in prices a great increase in the amount of live animals imported into Europe—from a value of $3,025,000 in 1870 to $40,650,000 in 1885. All this is true enough; but it is not fair to produce this set of figures and omit the equally striking figures with regard to the decrease in number of cattle grown in Europe itself. According to the Census enumerations of successive periods, we find the number of cattle for every 1,000 inhabitants to have been as follows:—

	Beeves.	Sheep.	Pigs.
1869	331	700	152
1880	302	568	140

Since 1880 there has been no general re-count, but there is every reason to believe that there has been an absolute diminution in the number of sheep in the face of an increase of population.

It is obvious that this may offset the increase in imports. The two sets of results are not in a form where they can readily be compared with one another. We can only quote Major Craigie's estimates as to the consumption of meat per head of population in the United Kingdom :—

1868	Lbs.	100·5
1872		109·2
1876		111·4
1880		114·1
1881		108·3
1882		103·3
1883[1]		111·6

This certainly shows no great tendency toward over-production. And in connection with Mr. Wells' statistics as to the growth of a particular form of meat trade, we may call attention to the fact that according to Neumann's estimate the total international trade in meat of all kinds had only increased from 1,946 million marks in 1877 to 1,954 millions in 1884.

WOOL.

Passing from food products to the raw material of clothing, let us take the history of wool. Here we find the same story as in the case of cotton. New processes had created an increased demand—one which the growers were hardly able to supply. The stocks in Europe at the end of the year 1880 were 207,000 bales; at the end of 1885, in spite of the increased production, they were only 180,000 bales. This does not look like over-production. It looks much more like the effort to supply an increased demand. Mr. Wells says that the increase in the world's production from 1860 to 1885 was 100 per cent., and from 1873 to 1885 20

[1] Major Craigie's last investigations seem to indicate a slight falling off in 1886-7 per capita, as compared with 1883.

per cent. This would make the increase from 1860 to 1873 67 per cent. Why should the comparatively small increase in the latter period have the effect on prices which he attributes to it? The only difference between wool and cotton seems to be that our statistics with regard to the former are not quite so complete, and therefore we cannot speak with so much confidence. The general indications with regard to the two articles seem much alike.

IRON AND COAL.

Nor can we regard Mr. Wells' facts as conclusive in the case of articles like iron and coal. It is true that the cost of production of these things has been somewhat lessened; but it is seriously open to question whether this reduction will account for the fall in price which has actually occurred. Nor can we accept Mr. Wells' statements of fact without challenge. He says that "in 1870 the average output of coal per miner in the British coal-mines (counting all the men employed) was 250 tons—an amount never before reached. In 1879 this amount had increased to 280 tons per man, and in 1884 the average for the five preceding years was reported at 322 tons." Mr. Wells does not quote his authority, so that we have not had the chance of verifying his statement directly, but bringing it into comparison with the reports of H.M. Inspectors of Mines, as quoted by Jeans and others, we find the following discrepancies:—

Year.	Product. Tons.	No. of men employed.	Av. output per man. Tons.	Output per man, as stated by Wells.
1870	110,400,000	350,900	314	250
1879	134,000,000	523,900	256	280
1880	146,800,000	537,800	273	—
1881	154,200,000	495,500	311	—
1882	156,500,000	504,000	311	—
1883	163,700,000	514,900	318	—
Average '79-83	151,000,000	515,200	293	322

Instead of an increase of 29 per cent., as indicated by Mr. Wells, we find a decrease of 7 per cent. in the output per man in 1879-83 as compared with 1870. Nor does the output per man for the years 1884 and 1885 appear to have maintained itself at the level of that of 1883; it is provisionally stated at about 309 tons for each year, and the tendency of the final corrections is to lower rather than increase the provisional figures. Of course Mr. Wells may have based his statements on other authorities than those to which we have access; but, in the absence of any definite citations, we are justified in letting these contradictions stand without further attempt to explain them.

With regard to iron the case is more complicated. We note, however, that Mr. Wells' statement of an increase of "about 100 per cent." from 1870 to 1886 is not justified. The figures on which he bases it do not bear out the statement; and if the necessary allowance is made for the incompleteness of the earlier returns, we find it still further from the truth. Sir Lowthian Bell's estimate of an increase from 14,345,000 tons in 1872 to 21,063,000 in 1883, or 47 per cent. in twelve years, is probably very near the truth. It should, however, be noted that the year 1883 represented a maximum, while 1872 did not. The world's production in 1884 and 1885 was much less than in 1883; and though the product of the United States for 1886 was very much greater than ever before, this fact cannot be used to explain the course of prices in 1884 and 1885.

It should be further noted that, while there has been an increased output per man, corresponding pretty accurately to this increase in product, the decline in prices has gone on much faster than the reduction in cost. In other words, while a single labourer produces 50 per cent. more iron (according to Mr. Wells' figures), the price of that iron has fallen so much that his aggregate product commands a very much smaller price than it did before. The facts are as follows :—

		Prices per ton.		
		America.	England.	Germany.
	World's Iron Product.	Anth'cite pig.	Clev'd No. 3.	Spiegeleisen.
Year.	Metric tons.	$	s.	rm.
1872	14,700,000	48·87	97·12	210
1882	21,300,000	25·75	43·5	72
1883	21,500,000	22·37	39·5	58
1884	20,200,000	19·87	37·0	55
1885	19,500,000	17·87	33·0	47

The decline in price has been so much greater than the improvement in efficiency, that some further explanation must be sought. Was there an over-production of the raw material beyond the requirements of the market? Mr. Wells thinks that there was, and introduces some evidence to support his view, but not nearly enough to make out a case; while he passes in silence over some important evidence on the opposite side.

The fall from 1873 to 1878 was special, concurrent with the panic in the United States and the contraction and liquidation in the commercial world subsequently. The amount of unsold stocks in the producers' hands increased during that period from 600,000 to 800,000 tons, on an aggregate American product of from 2,300,000 to 2,900,000, or from 25 to 50 per cent. of the whole. In recent years the aggregate American product has nearly doubled, but the unsold stocks run very much smaller—10 per cent. of the total instead of 25 or 30 per cent. This does not look as though production had been outrunning the needs of the world for actual use. In point of fact, the use of iron has increased enormously. Take one instance—the increase in the world's railroad mileage from 1871 to 1875, inclusive, was about 46,000 miles; from 1881 to 1885, inclusive, it was about 72,000 miles. This difference was more than proportionate to the relative increase in the iron product.

We reach the conclusion that though the cost of production of iron is less, prices have fallen to a greater extent than can be accounted for in this way; and that Mr. Wells fails to make out a case of real over-production as compared with consumers' needs.

There is one commercial staple of first-rate importance—namely, sugar—in which we think that Mr. Wells proves that there has been real over-production. If so, his success at this point is as damaging to his general line of argument as are his failures elsewhere. He himself admits that this over-production has been mainly due to an artificial stimulus by sugar bounties. Let us look at the bearing of this fact on the question at issue. He has set out to prove that the fall in prices is due to multiplication and cheapening of commodities, and that this in turn is due to man's increased control over productive forces. Taking the seven commodities which are probably the most important in his list —wheat, cotton, meat, wool, coal, iron, sugar—we find that in the first two there has been no over-production; that in the next four he has at any rate failed to prove his case; while in the seventh—the only one where the facts are on his side—he himself admits the existence of a special set of reasons, different from those with which we are immediately concerned. In six cases his facts are open to objections; in the seventh case, where the facts are right, they are totally inconclusive.

EFFECTS OF FALL IN PRICES UPON FIXED AND DEFERRED PAYMENTS.

There is one aspect of the question, as Mr. Wells presents it, which yet remains to be considered. What has been the effect of these changes upon the relative positions of debtors and creditors? Have prices fallen so rapidly as to make it harder to pay one's debts? or have the improvements in production more than counterbalanced this effect.

Money is not merely a medium of exchange or a measure of value of different things at the same time. It is also a standard of deferred payments. In modern commercial life this is perhaps its most important use. A has borrowed one thousand dollars of B in 1877. Will he in paying that same amount in 1887 virtually have to give back a great deal more than he received? Or A has leased some land of B at a fixed rental—will he in paying that rental have to give much more now than he was forced to give in 1873? This is the practical form in which the question of the appreciation of gold puts itself; except that, for the majority of men, the periods of payment are not so long, and the change covers a series of transactions rather than a single one. The advocate of the debtor class says that his client has to pay more, because the same number of dollars represents a larger amount of wheat or sugar, coal or iron, or almost anything which his client is likely to produce. The other side answers that he does not, because a given amount of sugar or iron is produced with correspondingly less labour; that while the amount of commodities representing the debt may be greater, the real cost as measured by human labour and human sacrifice has not increased in the same way; and that this cost of production is a fairer measure of steadiness of value than the mere amount of commodities of any kind. If he does not say this, he at any rate implies it.

We ought to premise that this is a question which, aside from the facts already cited and others of similar import, will never be put so entirely at rest that those who believe as Mr. Wells does cannot argue about it with a degree of plausibility to themselves. The books show that the same interpretation has by some been applied at every period of depression of prices the world has ever experienced, and has just this in its favour, that it is to an extent true of all of them. Industrial history is but a record of man's increasing power. Gradually he has been obtaining control of the forces of nature, ever seeking, and each succeeding decade more and more nearly securing, the growth of two blades of grass where one grew before. It is easy enough to say that the progression has been marvellous since this century began. At its very opening Whitney's cotton gin, Watt's steam-engine, Hargreaves and Arkwright's spinning machines, and the factory system simply re-created manufacture. From that point it has grown and expanded almost daily, concurrently with the spread of civilization and the opening up of new peoples to civilized habits and tastes, while giving to those peoples through a mutual interchange of commodities the power to gratify desires.

Now, why should the action of this principle culminate with 1873? Up to that date we had gone on in accord with John Stuart Mill's natural sequence, simply increasing the productive powers of the world, increasing the supply of commodities in the markets, and at the same stroke, and to the same extent, increasing purchasing power. All at once the natural operation of improved methods in production, according to this claim, absolutely changed the relation of things. Although prices since that date have fallen as never before, man's increased control over the productive forces of nature is held to account for it all; and the further assumption is boldly made, that a given expenditure of labour and capital will pay a debt of a given amount to-day as easily as it would a few years ago. While accepting neither proposition, let us for a moment notice the latter claim, as it includes both, and so many make much of it.

How, we would ask, can it be reconciled with the change in the position of capital? The difficulty in investing it in such a way as to obtain the same return per cent., which could readily be had a few years ago, is too obvious to be dwelt upon. How can it be urged, in view of the notable alteration in the position of the lessees of farms in Great Britain and Ireland? If their rent can be paid with the same expenditure of labour, why reduce it? Only a few years ago Irish rents were lowered on account of the obviously increased burden which a full payment imposed, and they were fixed judicially for fifteen years on what was believed to be a fair basis. Hardly was the settlement completed before a further fall in the prices of produce made the reduced rent as onerous as the original had been. How can we make this claim accord with the situation of debts due England by India and others due Europe by Egypt? Each of them was contracted when the prices of wheat, cotton, and the other products those people pay in were, some of them, 50 per cent. higher than now. How can the proposition be made to conform to the condition everywhere admitted in commercial circles, that the margin of profit in nearly every industry is so reduced that the return to the producer is very small indeed? In this narrow margin we have the basis of all the combinations and "trusts" that are being formed—they are merely the efforts of struggling industries to recover or save themselves by resisting the tendency of the times, and are consequently extending so as to include more and more departments of trade.

With regard to labour there seems at first sight more doubt, many maintaining that labourers have gained greatly by the recent fall in prices. Any grain of truth contained in this statement, if there be such, is confined to certain trades in this country, and due wholly to combinations which have been able, in a greater or less extent, to maintain wages in face of a tendency to decline. But those who urged this view must make it general in its application. Their argument is something like this: True, the labourer gets less wages per yard or per ton than he did a few years ago, but his efficiency has been so much increased that he makes about the same per day which he did before. Meantime the articles which he buys have fallen in price; he has therefore less expenditure and more available surplus.

WAGES AND EARNINGS.

Our previous remarks seem clearly enough to refute this claim. We may, however, suggest one condition without stopping to cite others which, even if the assumption could otherwise be established, would interfere with such reasoning. The chance for the labourer depends not on the amount he makes per day, but on the amount he makes per year. Suppose that a single labourer in a day produces fifty per cent. more goods. If the piecework price has fallen fifty per cent., he receives approximately the same wages as before. But sometimes the market will not take the whole additional stock of goods which would be produced if the labourer worked all the year through. The effect of the change in many instances has been not that the labourer produces more goods, and thus earns the same amount with the same labour, but simply that he produces the same amount of goods with less work and therefore less aggregate pay for the year, even though the amount received per day be the same.

Of all industrial statistics, those concerning time lost are among the most important, and at the same time the most difficult to obtain. We only know the general drift of the facts; but in many instances this is quite unmistakable. In the textile industries it shows itself in the increasing disinclination on the part of the manufacturers to run except for orders. In the manufacture of those articles of wearing apparel which are subject to definite seasons—the hat trade, for instance—the times of work are becoming shorter and shorter, the intervals of inactivity longer and longer.

But we are not quite confined to these general indications. The English figures furnish us indirectly with the ground for important inferences on this matter. Take those for iron, as quoted by Mr. Wells himself. If, as he says, the average product per man at the furnaces increased from 173 tons in 1870 to 261 tons in 1884, or 51 per cent., while the total product increased only from 5,962,000 tons in 1870 to 7,529,000 tons in 1884, or 26 per cent., it follows that the amount of employment in the iron industry must have decreased nearly one-fifth. The statistics of occupations give us no warrant for assuming that this change is due to diminished number of labourers seeking work; we are forced to the conclusion that it represents forced idleness on the part of a large number of them. The statistics of the British coal industry furnish the same general indications. The number of men employed in 1874 to produce 125,000,000 tons of coal was 539,000 ; in 1883 the product had increased to 164,000,000, but only 515,000 men were required to produce it. Yet there is reason to believe that the number of coal miners in 1883 was greater than in 1874, and that the difference in apparent number employed may be due to short time, rather than to the presence of any large number of hands who were completely out of work.

The United States Census figures for 1880 and 1870 are not without value in this matter. If we compare the statistics of occupations with those of manufactures we have a rough means of comparing the total number employed with the average number employed; and this furnishes a sort of indication as to the regularity of employment. In this connection we find that the total number (occupation table) employed in manufacturing, mechanical, and mining industries increased from 2,707,000 in 1870 to 3,837,000 in 1880, or 41 per cent. ; while the average number of hands employed by the manufacturers increased from 2,054,000 in 1870 to 2,733,000 in 1880, or only 33 per cent. The same ratio of increase is found in the detailed returns from the mines. But if the number of workmen was increasing faster than the amount of employment from 1870 to 1880, there is reason to believe that the further change in the same direction since 1880 has been much more marked. It is hardly too much to say that the facts with regard to efficiency of labour, on which Mr. Wells relies to explain the fall in prices, really indicate that the labourers are producing very much less than they might, and are therefore suffering from irregularity of employment.

CONCLUSION.

From whatever point of view we regard it, the attempt to prove that the existing fall of prices is unaccompanied by any appreciation of gold seems to fail distinctly. We may differ as to the inferences to be drawn, or as to the practical measures to be adopted, but we cannot shut our eyes to the fact that there has been a change in the conditions of currency of the world, and not merely in the conditions of production. We have unsparingly called attention to Mr. Wells' errors of fact, because we believe that his statements, if accepted, are likely to defeat his main purpose in writing the present series of articles. What will be the practical lesson which most people will draw from what Mr. Wells tells them? When he adduces arguments to show that currency questions have little or nothing to do with the present state of things, he simply urges them all the more strongly in the direction of artificial restrictions of the supply. Of one thing they are certain, and that is that prices have fallen. Whether they are going to fall any more neither Mr. Wells nor any one else can tell them. Of the future they know nothing. Of the present they know that under existing conditions it is a great deal harder to pay their debts, or to get any profit on their capital, not to speak of fully employing their labourers, than it was fifteen years ago. They know, if they will look at the facts, that artificial stimulus by positive bounties has failed. The attempt to increase production does more harm than good. If, then, the matter is one which is solely and squarely a question of production and not of exchange, they see but one thing left. The supply must be restricted.

Their control over the productive forces of nature they find illusory, unless they can control the same thing in the hands of other people as well as themselves; whether by trusts or by a high tariff is a matter of indifference. What will be the outcome of this tendency it is as yet too soon to predict. But it is at least open to question whether the advocates and supporters of currency restriction are not playing into the hands of those who advocate and practise restriction of trade. There is no one who would deprecate this result more strongly than Mr. Wells. Freedom of production has no more vigorous or successful champion than he. His last article in the series, on Government Interference, is admirable, both in its facts and its lessons. For the sake of what is strongest in Mr. Wells' position, we deem it important to correct some of his errors with regard to prices. For if he, under a misapprehension of the facts, persuades his readers that the monetary standard has nothing to do with the present depression, they will rush to the conclusion that free competition of producers is wholly responsible for it, and will act accordingly.

THE END.

Richard Clay & Sons, Limited, London & Bungay.

www.ingramcontent.com/pod-product-compliance
Lightning Source LLC
Chambersburg PA
CBHW020905230426
43666CB00008B/1317